REFLECTIONS ON THE LAKE

Living Seven Years on Lake Tanganyika

VICTORIA HUWILER-FINDLAY

Cover design by Mapalo Mutale

Editing and typeset Write Lake Ltd

Write Lake Ltd

33B Mpulungu Rd, Olympia Park

Lusaka

Zambia

www.writelake.com

ISBN 978-9982-70-998-9

Victoria Huwiler-Findlay

Email: victoriahuwiler@gmail.com

REFLECTIONS ON THE LAKE

TABLE OF CONTENTS

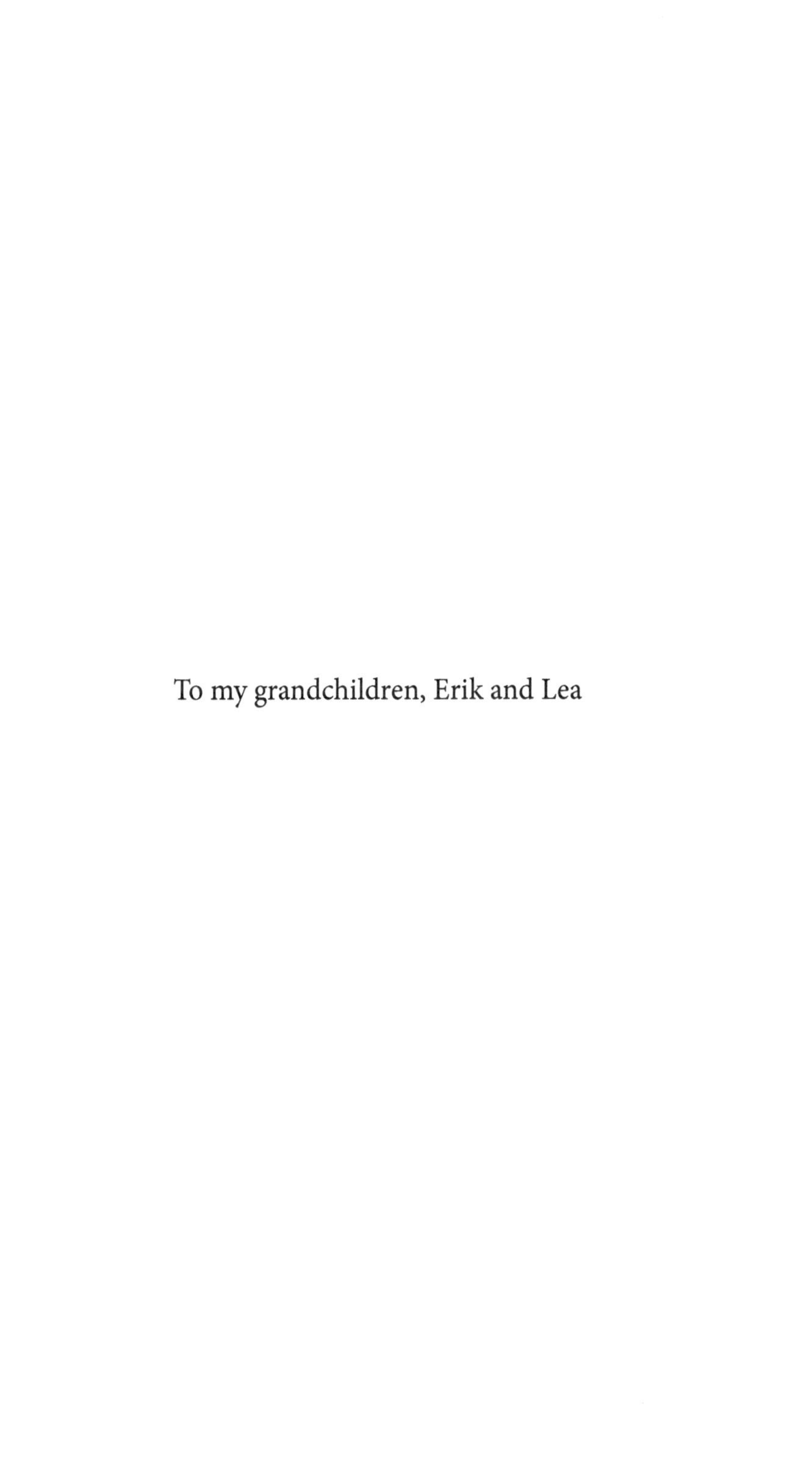

To my grandchildren, Erik and Lea

PROLOGUE

This short book is a collection of my notes, stories, and monthly diary, sometimes my annual accounts, living on the lake. I wrote notes, occasionally articles, other times stories of people and events, recording daily, more often monthly or by season. I wrote my experiences and reflections on Lake Tanganyika.

Putting this together after seven years, I felt that it was easier to change it to past tense rather than the present tense in which the diary was originally written. My writing was haphazard too. I'd sometimes write a story about someone or an event that happened that had touched me. Other times, I recorded information about the lake monthly. In compiling all this into one book, my story can be at times unconnected, incoherent and a mixture of styles. In my attempts to conform to well-known structures, the book seemed to lose its charm, authenticity and spontaneity. So left to my own devices, we have notes, stories, articles, letters, reflections, thoughts, and experiences. They are pieces of pain, laughter and learning as I grew in-depth, understanding and hopefully wisdom while I spent seven years on the lake.

LIVING ON THE LAKE

The Year I Arrived, 2014

This unusual site, villages nosing in their stately manner, unique, deserted except for the occasional fishing boat and the fishermen selling kapenta, buka buka, nkupi, and Nile perch (the fish of Lake Tanganyika).

I had come back to the homes of my mother and grandmother. I now lived in the Northern province, close to Abercorn, where my parents married. My other house was in Chinsali, where my grandmother met her husband, Jack Goddard. Little did I understand at the time, the meaning of growing roots.

I came to Mpulungu, Tukulungu, my new home, simply because of the sheer beauty of the lake, Lake Tanganyika. The opportunity came, the lake called me, and I chose to live here. My life before this was hosting investors into the country, driving them nationwide, on a crusade to bring investment and employment to the less fortunate. The bonus, of course, for me, was a hope for one lucrative deal after which I could retire.

I don't think the lucrative deal I imagined ever manifested, but I did find my Shangri La. An Englishman, Toby Veall, had settled in Zambia on the lake. He sold aquatic fish for cichlids hobbyists. I was told he was tough, hardcore, loud, often abusive, and would not take nonsense from anybody. His manager, a South African, got tired of being yelled at and told to 'f.... off.' One day, as they sat on the deck drinking beer, he pushed Toby into the water in a playful and vindictive manner. Unfortunately, he directly hit on a heap of rocks. Toby ended up paralysed and in a wheelchair for the rest of his life. He returned to Wales. His lake paradise crumbled, falling to pieces in its desire to return to dust.

When I was first brought here, it felt like the place had called me, had drawn me here. Soon after this visit, Toby got my email address and phone number and started calling me to negotiate a sale. I didn't need much convincing. I felt that the place was mine, like I had searched for this for a long time. I always wanted to live by the water. I had two small holiday homes at the time, one on the Kafue River and the other on the Mulungushi dam. I loved the water and wanted to be near it, to be able to swim every day in nature and not the artificial pools we had become accustomed to.

I wanted to bathe in nature, know her, understand her, perhaps purify myself from false perceptions, the superficial lifestyle I'd been living. I wanted to comprehend life at its deepest level and instinctively felt water had that purifying, cleansing power. This place provided the opportunity, the dream I'd always had. I wanted to be a part of Mpulungu and, most of all, the lake.

Besides, sometimes having a bunch of hooligans at the height of the kapenta season, screaming fishermen, nets being pulled in, there were no alarming dispatches of tourists. Although sometimes the horrors of tourist invasions can be a distraction, we could have done with more tourists, more activities and jobs for the people. Jobs were desperately needed. The poverty was shocking. The backwardness. The isolation. It appeared to me, they lived and existed in their own time zone, wholly detached from the modern world.

The women here reminded me of granny, her sisters and cousins. They were far from the madding crowd, lost in their world and time. They were simple, poor, kind, loving, charming, lost to the madness of city life and urban development. A world, it appeared to me, they didn't crave. Some villagers had never ventured into Mbala, the nearest town from the lake. Some children had never seen Mpulungu, they lived in one of the remotest parts of Zambia. There was no road access here. They had lost sense of time. It seemed that they were living in their own time capsule 200 years ago. There were possibilities of girls marrying at thirteen, never travelling, fishing in the fishing season, then moving to the hills to farm when the rains appeared. I loved the place.

Waves shuffled across the lake, sharply defined by the glare of the sun. What was missing was friends, good company, development, schools, clinics; the poverty broke my heart. The expressions of burnt, black faces of men, patient and resigned to their fate of mealie meal and fish. Women were comfortable being at home and uninterested in employment, perhaps because they knew there was none but never asked. Though I loved the people dearly, they reminded me of my grandmother. I decided not to be too naïve and nostalgic. I realised they were trained in the art of deception, their faces always cheerful and smiling as things disappeared behind my back. Although they spoke Lungu, a Bemba dialect, the memories of my granny floated back as I mingled with these people on the lake, The Lungu, the place, Tukulungu.

A boat trip into Mpulungu

'This could be turned into a bustling place, rampant chic

restaurants, cafes, bistros. Instead, all I saw were sweating faces over metal plates and jugs, serving nshima, chicken, T-bone and frozen bream brought in by Capital Fisheries, which was imported from China and Thailand. Good God, what a shame,' I complained to my new friends, Martin and Joyce, at Waterfront Mpulungu. They ran the pub and grill overlooking the lake.

'Stalls of all sizes, all selling the same thing— tomatoes, onions, rape, cabbage, beans.'

I got the attention of the pub. They all laughed.

'Where are the avocados, the paw-paws, the pineapples, the carrots, the beetroot, the lettuce, these are all over the cities? What's happened to Mpulungu?' The laughter got louder.

'You're a breath of fresh air.' A stranger laughed.

'Is it lack of imagination, creativity or pure laziness?'

I enjoyed the attention I was getting. I hoped to cultivate friendships too. I was from Lusaka and needed to make new friendships and acquaintances. After all, I was a city girl, and the solitude was getting the better of me.

Little did I understand that all the soils in Mpulungu were beach soils. Most of the produce was grown in Mbala, a thirty-minute drive away. It was much higher and cooler than Mpulungu. Many people working in Mpulungu lived in Mbala because of the heat and humidity of Mpulungu. They preferred the freshness of Mbala.

The market in Mpulungu looked like it needed an army of brooms to sweep the mess, casualties of vegetable leaves, bananas, plastic bags, tins, and unidentified mangled mash were littered everywhere. Stalls of varying sizes, crates upside down, cardboard boxes, wispy clamps of paper, baskets, bags, floor garnished with trash, all waiting to be washed away in one big Mpulungu storm.

'The government has forgotten us; they don't care about us here in the rural areas. All they worry about is stuffing their own pockets. Their bank accounts are full of money while us in the rural areas, we suffer, we suffer, Madam, here we suffer.'

Another stranger joined in, 'There's no development here, we, we, we want to see development, *buyantanshi*, development, we need a future, we need development.'

Jokingly, I continued, 'We need clinks and murmurs from the

lounges, the beaches, the cafes, clinks of glasses and murmurs of pleasure. The place has so much potential.'

Everyone laughed.

'My daughter coined it, Lake Tanganyika—the crowning jewel of Zambia. We should play on this, bring the tourists. This will bring jobs, entertainment. It would bring the people with the money here, then perhaps development would follow.' I blurt out.

I broke into the easy buddy banter with the people. I felt accepted as a kindred spirit. At the same time, living remote, privileged, isolated. A guest once left behind a written reminder in my guest book, 'we should replace the expression of 'living like a king in Paris' to 'living like a queen on Lake Tanganyika.' Comparatively, I was spoilt and the guilt sunk in. The guilt came from the pain of so much poverty at the mercy of all the blatant corruption going on in the upper echelons. I wanted to make a difference, leave a legacy, and do something for the less fortunate but to stay away from politics. Criticism of the politicians in power was never tolerated in this country. The music blasted in my ears, breaking my thoughts. It was impossible to talk.

‘Could you put the music down for a while? It’s getting unbearable here and impossible to talk,’ I addressed the barman. He was in charge of the cassettes, and his choice of music was rhumba from Congo.

‘Us Africans Madam, we like noise, we like music. If I don’t play loud music, people come here and complain. They say, “there’s no life here, where’s the life?” So I have to play loud music.’ He then started dancing.

I sped off in my speed boat, the pelican. It had a new sixty horsepower mercury engine, which I had just bought from Autoworld. The music screaming at me as I escaped. The year was 2014.

On my way home, my thoughts lingered as to why there seemed to be so much noise everywhere you travelled in Zambia. Loud music, dancing, particularly, drunkenness along with the music. A reminder, to me, of the loss of soul connection, a continent raped of soul and spirit, a white man’s dream left in its place. They left behind their idea of development, technology, as an aspiration for happiness. We took money and development to mean an assurance of happiness and the way to go.

1964 was the year of our independence. Now more than 50 years on, what manifested instead was disillusionment. Where was the development, the future promised, the happiness proclaimed? As for the church, we spoke of Jesus and a Christian nation, but the reality was an obsession with power, money, corruption and black magic. In addition, there was this total disregard and disrespect for the poor. The villages and slums drowned their sorrows in loud music and alcohol, their escape, their happiness.

They were given no other forms of recreation, sport, drama, theatre, positive recreation. Instead, alcohol, sex, dancing, marijuana, entertainment and relaxation, brought the feeling of ease. To drown in your sorrows, it had to be loud music. The louder, the better. It shut down the pain.

An hour away was Tukulungu, my new home. The place was an open season for nature lovers, and each month brought a treat of its own. I curled under the wild fig tree that canopied my home. The figs were now overripe and sweetened by the October summer sun. This season also brought with it an atrium of chirping birds, an orchestra singing above the thatched roof of my home. I lived in the heart of nature and had time to think, contemplate, reflect and to simply learn what nature would offer me, what these people would bring to me.

My daily view was emerald green waters with monkeys trespassing with their newly borns clutched in their arms. Bush babies screamed at night like little human babies. There were garden snakes hiding under rocks or in trees keeping away from the burning heat. A forest cobra, going to sleep in my thatched roof, left alone, not to be disturbed, I was taught, a new learner to this world, I became. Red-winged starlings nestled in my lounge. I dived into the warm waters of the lake, which ranged between 25-27 degrees all year round. The warm lake was an invitation to swim.

Here I discovered cichlids that dominate the lake, a very unusual species of fish, all with their subtle colours and distinct behaviour. These mouth brooding species of cichlids, so unusual. It attracted a lot of hobbyists and researchers eager to explore. I felt invited too, to explore the mysteries of Lake Tanganyika. I discovered the wonders of Kapembwa, the goddess, the donna fish, the mermaid of Lake Tanganyika, the spirit that had called me, invited me into her domain.

Mpulungu, Tukulungu, all the way to the Tanzanian border. Chipwa, the two villages, Chipwa Zambia and Chipwa Tanzania, were separated by the Kalambo River and divided by the colonials, one side Northern Rhodesia, the other side, German Tanganyika. One side English imposed, the other side

German enforced. The river, two meters apart at its closest, and 4-6 metres its widest, divided by language, culture and administration, a separation to last forever.

At independence, Julius Nyerere chose to make Swahili the official language of Tanzania. Kenneth Kaunda decided on English as our lingua franca. The divide between the two countries widened. Zambians spoke relatively good English nationwide while the Tanzanian English deteriorated. The villages living on the border continued to be united through tribe. These were all Lungu people living here, they spoke Lungu and their traditions remained the same. They married each other, despite living in different countries. No one respected the border posts in love relationships unless it came to fishing in each other's territory, here the divide showed itself. Zambians or Tanzanians accused each other of stealing fish and reported to their respective authorities.

I romanticised my slice of paradise. I sketched a bright future in my mind, what it could look like. I drew models and sketches in my mind, similar to what was done to Livingstone. I envisioned tarred roads, clean streets, flamboyants and jacarandas canopying the streets, bougainvillaea to add to the splash of colour. The pavements were repaired, freshly painted buildings, hawkers placed in creatively built-up markets and cultural villages created. Billboards professionally displayed, unlike the graffiti thrown over every wall in the cities, towns, and villages by the mobile networks Airtel, Zamtel, and MTN. Their kindergarten colours of red, yellow and green define the walls of vintage buildings. The old golf club in Kasama is painted in Zamtel's deep green brand colours, and it's shocking to the soul.

Mpulungu was small and beautiful enough, delightful, a challenge, realistic, something special and unique. It could be created into a model to inspire the rest of the country.

I heard the sound of the crickets swelling, approving my wild thoughts.

7 AUGUST 2014

The Contract with Julius

Julius came from Lake Victoria. He was Tanzanian with a reputation of being the best boat maker that Mpulungu had ever seen. He had all his certifications and credentials from Lake Victoria. He was to repair my fibreglass boats and wooden dhow that came with purchasing the property. My wooden dhow was called The Shalom, meaning peace in Hebrew.

When Toby heard the name it had been given by the manager after his departure, his response was, 'What a fag, who the hell calls his boat, Shalom!' I rather liked the name, probably because it was more feminine. Shalom sounded mystical to me, and perhaps more about my purpose here, The Shalom it remained.

The boats were now all damaged. Toby had been away for nearly six years and things began to break down and deteriorate. The Shalom was full of leaks. The fibreglass boats needed refurbishing, reinforcing where the engines were held. They all looked like they needed a good coat of paint.

There was another dilapidated boat staring at me, ready for the dump. They called it The Tamba. Toby brought it in from Mongu, Western Province. I was about to place it on the dump heap when Julius looked at it. He excitedly promised me he could make it right.

'Six weeks from now, 28 November,' he said, 'you can pick up all your boats.'

It all sounded promising. We agreed on US$5,700 to repair all the boats, which sounded like a fair deal. The first three weeks went well. I pulled all the boats in a convoy using The Shalom leading the way and different guys in each boat. Thomas, my coxswain and key staff member, was with me in the Shalom. I was excited as it felt like a whole new life for me.

Julius was an excellent worker, but I didn't realise that he had different contracts with so many other people needing their boats refurbished. He constantly demanded for more money, and after four weeks, he had taken the full US$5,700. I was super eager to get the job done and continued dishing out more cash. However, every week there was a new excuse for more money. Once he received the full amount, he disappeared.

He ran away leaving two boats untouched. The pelican he had repaired had an even bigger crack than the one he fixed, perhaps caused by dropping it. He was probably skimping on labour. The boats are heavy and need a lot of manpower to carry. He must have tried some shortcut and dropped the boat. I arrived to find the boat abandoned, sitting in the wrong place, two boats untouched and one repaired but with a glaring crack. The boatman had taken a dive and was nowhere to be found. What a lesson!

October 2014

Dear Georgie, I wrote to one of my dearest friends in London. In fact, my longest friend, we met when I was only seven years old.

Living in a remote location, I found writing mail a fine treat.

I just did my weekly shopping and took a trip into Mpulungu, where I get all my supplies. It is an hour boat ride from here, far from your markets of surplus, variety, excessive, hygienic and spotless routine. Here we need an army of brooms to sweep up the mess, scraps of fallen vegetables, plastic, a floor garnished with tomatoes, onions, cabbage, rape, impwa, garden eggs, you call them, bananas, paw-paw, and other undefined scraps.

I didn't have time to finish the letter, and it lay there in note form. Then, someone called me, and my mind got distracted.

The year came to an end, and I did not have time to get back to the letter. My style had always been to scribble on a piece of paper, then later transfer it to an email, booklet, short story, or an article to be published. My desk was always piled with notes that I'd file or put away, and usually at some point in my life, I often returned to these notes either to throw away or to complete.

I spent most of my time scribbling words for my brochure, the website and planning menus. In December, I wrote:

Secret spots, Kalambo Falls Lodge, and continued: You'd be hard-pressed to find a place more remote than Tukulungu, home of the Lungu people, the indigenous people living around the Kalambo River. It was an hour boat trip from Mpulungu on my hand-built wooden dhow.

As a former businesswoman and shareholder of Roma Park, I packed my bags and furniture into a canter. I hit the road for the bush in my Isuzu van, overloaded with food, supplies and wine.

Friends joked and mocked me as they waited to witness my return. Instead, the place grew on me. The hidden secrets of Kapembwa, the goddess of the lake, are considered sacred. Her bed could be viewed directly opposite my lounge-dining area and on a clear day. I could see the site from my open bedroom. My room opened to all of nature. I had no curtains or windows. I lived with nature in her bowel, separated only by a thin mosquito net to keep the bats and bugs away from my body as I slept. Like my cats, I purred into the night.

The little known surrounding bays had pristine beaches still undiscovered by the tourist industry. It was my answer to our tropical island dreams and so close to the home where my mother had grown up, Abercorn, now Mbala. It had perfect, clean, quiet beaches, endemic flora and fauna, vervet monkeys to greet you every morning, with bush babies screaming for attention at night. A tropical island fantasy, the beauty of it unexploited, 'a place in the sun.'

I kept the lodge entirely eco-friendly, going further to explore its mysteries and turned it into a scientific research centre and *maison d'autres* to give it that *je ne sais quoi* I was looking for. It was a gem for snorkelling lovers because of the emerald green waters and the awe-inspiring variety of cichlids.

You could camp on isolated beaches and feast on the fresh fish or the catch of the day. The idyllic way of exploring the area was on our handmade wooden dhow, The Shalom—peace. I wrote through most of the days. That's what the place brought me, peace.

Something strange happened to time here. I spent my days swimming, snorkelling, reading, having beach picnics, open log fires, and experimenting with the local cuisine. I heightened the local cuisine to international standards, *bondwe* in white wine, an amaranthus leaf widely eaten in Zambia, beans in a date and coconut sauce, nshima topped with mushrooms and served with village chicken, an organic pig or goat bought from the local villages. Pork marinated in salt, pepper with lots of garlic and rosemary, rubbed in oil and then slowly grilled in a smoker I designed. It was a simple open oven built with red brick and a wire tray placed across the centre. I could bake bread, roast and smoke fish, pork or goat. I created miracles with produce supplied by the villagers.

Although I remained vegetarian, I ate only vegetables, fruit, nuts, grain, fish, seafood, and lake fish. I stayed far away from pork, beef and chicken. I still cooked for my guests mainly Swiss, Germans and Austrians, who loved their meat.

I placed a hammock and propped up umbrellas on the beach, where I spent most of my time scribbling more notes. I watched the local fishermen in their hand-carved wooden boats with sails made from old mealie meal and cement bags. In fact, anything plastic was cut up and sewn into a sail. They glided to the shore, fresh fish from their day catch they brought in.

For that particular day, I'd lost my taste for the catch after spending an hour that morning snorkelling and admiring the beautiful spiralling swim of schools of fish. My taste for eating fish retreated for that day, preferring to contemplate living here forever.

It was already close to Christmas, so I thought it best to write one letter to my friends.

Dear Georgie, Gay, Renuka and Russell,

You've all become so special to me. Stuck here with waves shuffling across the lake, I think of you a lot. What's missing here is friends, company and companionship. I love the place. The expressions on the burnt black faces of men— patient and resigned. I only have men working here;

the women are complacent in the village and rarely come here asking for employment. The people are resigned to their fate and their simple diet of nshima and fish.

Though I love them dearly, things do tend to disappear. They seem to be so well trained in the art of deception, their faces always so cheerful and smiling, while things disappear behind my back.

I don't speak the language, Lungu, a kind of Bemba-Swahili dialect, I presume. They're surrounded by Bemba speaking people in Zambia and Swahili from Tanzania. God knows where I've landed. Our favourite connecting words are, 'super,' when they've done something right, and oh no, when it's a mistake. Fortunately, a lot of supers!

The place is an open season for nature lovers and each month brings a treat of its own. October is the height of summer with the heat comes a huge bird festival. We have an orchestra of birds that come to feast on the ripening fruit from the fig tree, which canopies my home. The rains have now begun.

I dive into those emerald green waters and spy on the cichlids which dominate the lake, with their subtle colours and marine behaviour. You'd swear this was the sea—a feast for the soul. The warm waters all year round, clearly, an invitation to swim every day, it's soul-inspiring, I can't get enough of this place.

I'm working on the kitchen and the cuisine, it's fine dining, so I'm inviting you all to come and visit. Bring those clinks and murmurs into my dining room and approvals of fine food.

It's strange the guests who come here. Generally, the women love the subtle finishes while the men appreciate the functional finishes, the boats, the homemade oven, the engines and the generators, the solar systems. The women comment on the food and the lovely dinner sets I've accumulated over the years.

I've become addicted to this place. I need friends to come and visit!

I had to end the letter abruptly. My attention turned to all the problems of the boats and engines. The Shalom was full of leaks. Some boatmen from Miyambe village were waiting for me outside, planning to take me to their worksite.

I was intrigued by the craftsmen, their skill, tools and provisions seemed so basic, yet the boats they carved out seemed so impressive. I felt the need to support them and immediately planned to buy the brand new wooden dhow they were making from hard dark indigenous wood, most of which I recognised as mukwa.

I started conjuring ideas of decking the boat to create an area for two, place a mattress, a hatchet to store food and drink, and another for fuel. The idea was to do an expedition on the lake and enjoy every bay along the way. First, I'd start with the Zambian side from Chipwa on the Tanzanian border to Ndole Bay until I touched the Congolese border and then return.

On the same day, I was visited by an entourage of very serious-looking men from Chitili village.

'We're here to have a meeting with the owner,' the sternest of them said. He had a piece of paper with him, a letter. A letter I've kept to date, on it was written:

Sichone James, D/H/T, Chitili preschool, 0974921552
George Sikazwe
Mashaka Mwinamanz

1. *Village headman Mr Happy Chikoye 0979002676*
2. *Indunas of headman Simon Musukuma*
3. *Gipsoni Yamba Secretary*
4. *Victor Simtowe*

5. *C. Siluyize*
6. *Goodson Kauga, no phone*

Still new to the place, I wondered what I had done, everyone was serious.

'Can I help you, sir?' I asked, still surprised.

It turned out that the meeting was to inform me that I was assisting Miyambe village and that they had also heard that I'd donated to the kindergarten. I was firmly told that the land I was on was provided for by Chitili village. If I was going to promote any project, it had to be in Chitili and not Miyambe village.

Miyambe village had apparently started to boast that I was supporting them. I supported a small village school, with 80 pupils, all between four and seven years old. I found that they were forty children in one class, with two teachers, whose salaries were paid by donations provided by parents. It was such an inspiring project that I'd assisted them with chairs, pens, pencils and a few other items.

It seemed so petty. I employed most of my staff from Chitili, I bought all my building materials from them, river sand, building sand, stones, chickens, goats, pigs, any fruit or vegetables they could supply me with. I took all the fish, good God, the pettiness of the whole meeting. But I smiled, tried to explain myself, and promised to commit to Chitili village. It was my lesson in village politics. I needed their support and confidence in me, so I'd have to be very careful how I trod.

Time had gone so fast, the year was up, and in its place 2015. I welcomed it as a virgin, unspoiled, clean, a new page, a new story, hope of something new and exciting.

END JULY - MID-AUGUST 2015

Harry

I arrived home from my annual European trip to find a massacre of trees. That's what it appeared to me at the time. Trees screaming, branches torn, some stumped, others turned into stools or footsteps on the ground. Fifty-year-old trees, now stumps, 100-year-old branches, lying on the floor, devastation is what it looked and felt like.

My eyes met the sunset and filled with tears. It smelt like blood, the sap oozing from torn branches. The staff resigned to dictates from the white *muzungus.* They were unable to advise. They were probably afraid of being fired.

The group from Basel had arrived, only four of them, thank God. The place was a mess nothing was ready for the group of twelve still to come. I had just flown in from Europe and hired a car to Mpulungu. My yellow double cab, Isuzu, had broken down just outside Kapiri Mposhi, between Kapiri Mposhi and Mkushi. I travelled for at least three days from Nice to London to Johannesburg to Lusaka to Mpulungu.

I arrived to an empty pantry in the kitchen. There was nothing prepared for dinner. Fortunately, I had stopped over to do a significant amount of shopping in Shoprite, Kasama. I dashed into the kitchen and started preparing a meal for six people. I served dinner and chatted to the new students. However, inside I squeezed the pain and volcano brewing, it was not the warm welcome I expected.

The place was returning to its usual self, the warm, spicy welcome of cinnamon in the pumpkin soup and incense burning on my miniature *mbaula* (brazier). I brought the incense from Chinsali where it was mined in streams and pools of water. I tried hard to stay calm and positive, searching for the good that might come out of this incident.

The morning was worse. I cringed at the piled up leaves, in some places they were a metre high, cans, bottles, paper, and plastic were everywhere. The dogs started jostling with each other, anticipating their daily walk. They could sense a war path and they got excited.

The rustling, falling leaves, branches everywhere. There was grass everywhere, as well as, from the unfinished thatching. The rooms were filthy, dusty shelves, cushions thrown upside down, or the wrong way round, it didn't matter, everything was a mess. Crumpled, twisted, squashed, tables, chairs, side tables, coffee tables in all directions, the sense of symmetry, harmony, gone wrong. *Does he notice it*, I wondered, *or is he simply blind?*

The words of the headman, Happy, came to mind, 'The spirits have gone. They've gone to Tanzania. We don't respect them here, so they've run away and we have no luck anymore here. All the luck has gone to Tanzania and other countries, where they respect the spirits.' *Are the spirits of my private forest about to flee*? I speculated. They'd been given no respect.

The long, graceful stems of the palms whipped around wildly unprotected by the trees they had once hidden behind. They were protected against the violent Lake Tanganyika winds. The winds clawed at the last leaves left on the trees and sent them flying onto the bed of flattened ferns from the incomplete fallen thatch roof.

I loved the cover of trees. It gave me a sense of privacy, secrecy and mystery in my remote life. I enjoyed this privilege, having lived a very public life in the past. But without the trees, I felt stripped naked and exposed. The heat was more intense. The wind roared, wilder than I ever remembered. From a distance the fishermen peeked into my life.

I could feel the gaze of the fisherman intruding in my life. Once in their traditional simplicity, non-intrusive, floating in the distance as they peeped through the leaves and branches that shielded me, now their gaze bothered me.

I yelled at the boy. I yelled but his soft, gentle nature calmed me down. He was only trying to please me but was out of his depth. He was new and fresh to the African bush. He was kind and gentle.

The branches would grow and the jungle would return. Some trees died leaving room for young ones to take over and new life to begin. He was only helping. I consoled myself.

The next day, Happy arrived to confirm the coming of the chief from Mbala, Chief Zombe. We planned to invite him for Independence Day on 24 October 2015. We needed beers and soft drinks served. There were requests for help and donations for the school. The day ended with laughter and jokes and the realisation of just how much I loved the place.

The trees would grow again.

APRIL - NOVEMBER 2015

Peter

It was April 2015, the last month of the rains in Mpulungu, when Peter came into my life. A naive socialist.

We were both revivals in our adventuring stage, like innocent students on their gap year. We were both excited about exploring the wild side of life, adventuring on wooden dhows across the lake to Kigoma, camping and hopping on mini-buses. We were both alone, our children grown up and we were ready for the seclusion, intimacy, passion and adventure.

My daughter Angelika and her partner Tue came to visit. Accompanying them was Tue's business partner Niels and his girlfriend, Alexandria. Peter was Alexandria's father.

Peter's first impression was that I had locked myself in isolation, a recluse, distanced myself from others, from life and he questioned the possibilities of me meeting a partner unless, of course, that's what I'd chosen.

My reply was straightforward, 'If it's meant to be, he'll find me here in Mpulungu. I travel a lot; relationships are acts of faith, accidents, Cupid's arrow, some mysterious agreement that could happen anywhere.'

Lost in this perfect paradise, he fell like a log, flat on his face, smitten by the ambience and presence of a woman, "ballsy," he called me.

The young ones, Tue, Angelika, Neils and Alexandria, took the hike to Kalambo Falls in the morning. They returned earlier than I had expected and just in time for lunch. I planned nkupi fish marinated in garlic, ginger, turmeric, lemon grass, fresh chilli, lemon leaves from my garden, lemon juice, cumin seed, and coconut milk served with cumin rice, jeera rice.

I had all the ingredients laid out, Bernard the chef pounding the garlic and ginger in my small African pestle, *kabende*, we called it. I moved to the kitchen, he followed me like a puppy. He was smitten. Sometimes I wondered if I went to the toilet would he follow, just like my kids had done when they were young, to the kitchen and bathroom they followed like little lambs.

On the couch by the fireplace, Peter followed, sitting on the steps, trying hard to capture my gaze, which I returned. I had been alone for ten years but enjoyed my freedom and space.

The food I cooked was orgasmic, my intimate private life, certainly not. Peter returned six weeks later for a month, and later in October, for more time, spending his time gazing at me in silence, singing love songs he prepared to me, a collection he had put together, especially for me. He came off as a dreamy, impractical socialist, a permanent cigarette between his fingers. He smoked 40 – 60 cigarettes a day, which led to a persistent cough. He drowned himself in smoke.

I wondered whether the smoking was an escape from pain or past suffering. Peter was sheltered and hid behind the hurt, the pain, whatever it had been, I tried to dig into his childhood and private life, searching for answers. He resisted and withdrew. The smoking intensified.

The guests arrived, the Swiss and the Austrians from Basel University, my biggest nightmare, his escape. Peter spent early mornings with the Swiss, late nights with the youngsters. He was withdrawn in his private pain. He curled up in the corner of his bed, intimacy and connection falling apart.

This was a man who confessed his love to every stranger. He hugged and kissed me publicly. On his last night, I had him close, feeling the closeness. The proximity and intimacy frightened him. Fear set in and he withdrew. He attempted to dash away for a *fag*. I wouldn't allow him to escape to the guests. I held him tight.

He told me he had been an alcoholic or was an alcoholic from the age of about 28-38, ten years of his life. Bottles of vodka to disguise the smell, anything alcoholic. Finally, he made up his mind to stop. He took to Diet Coke and cigarettes as his substitute.

With the youngsters, he could feel young again, even the mention of age, he curled and twisted inside. He wanted so desperately to prove something to me. The heated enclosure of glances, his naive optimism, he wallowed in it. Often tears in his eyes, glowing, blue, Scandinavian eyes. He was always eager to please. With the harsh blow of the hammering sun on his already burnt face, I knew I must not kill his enthusiasm.

I squeezed him and let him know it was all right, but he had to work on his smoking. We were out in the bush and medical assistance was non-existent. We only had a small clinic in Chisanza, 20 minutes away. It was manned by a male nurse,

Simon.

One hour away was Mpulungu and then there was the hospital in Mbala. You needed to be fit and healthy to live in the bush. Our lives depended on it. You really couldn't be eating away at your health with daily packets of cigarettes. The two did not go together.

'I promise, next time will be better. I'm torn between San Francisco, where I live now, and here. I know I want to be here, this is my future, but I still have a lot of things I need to sort out. I'm back for Christmas and New Year, hopefully forever in April 2016. I'm committed and I love you deeply. Next time, I promise,' Peter said. His eyes fiercely fixed to mine, holding me close to him. He left on 11 November, hoping to spend a few days with his daughter in Lusaka before jetting back home on the Emirates flight.

November 2015

It was a year later that I finally found a local boatman called Morgan who lived in the nearby village, Miyambe. He worked with a team of other boatmen. None of them had any qualifications or certification but what they had was a lifetime of experience working with their fathers. They helped their fathers build and repair boats. Leaks were patched up with cotton wool, using palm oil as lubrication. We then took a trip into Mpulungu, searching for oil paint for my Shalom. You took what you got here, bright coloured yellow and blue, all primary colours. The preference of the area, shining, sparkling, bright colours, which I soon grew fond of. It gave the place its special character. The boat stood out in bright, deep, primary blue and yellow. We used old shade cloth for the roof that we tore away from the ponds that were falling and fading. I'd planned a prettier roof and planned to bring a carpenter down from Lusaka to design something original, but as time passed, I got accustomed to the roof with palms, old mealie bags and rotting shade cloth. It seemed to fit in with the setting.

A few weeks later, Morgan arrived to tell me about an incomplete boat they had constructed in Miyambe. The person who had ordered the boat disappeared and the villagers were looking for a new buyer. To my delight, the boat was well designed and being incomplete, I could add my own flair to it. I decided on adding a deck, a dining area and create a space, like a hatchet, where I could place a double bed mattress. We also created a storage area for food and drinks and another on the other end of the boat for fuel, oils, and tools. I was hoping to get it ready for Christmas as a present for Peter when he returned. The idea was to do an expedition along the lake coast, from the

Tanzanian to the Congolese border. I wanted us to explore the Zambian shoreline. It was exciting times. I was overwhelmed and delighted with all my thoughts and plans for the new boat.

With the kwacha depreciating, Morgan initially quoted K16,000. With the additional deck and added refurbishments, the bill came up to K23,000 about US$2,300. Finally, I could have my own branded new wooden dhow. The deal was done, it seemed so inexpensive, everyone was happy, it was a win-win situation. The boat arrived but not in time for Christmas. It came months later and as agreed, the final payment was made upon delivery. It looked fine and grand. I was eager to go out on my expedition and try the boat out.

I bubbled with excitement as the boat sailed into the jetty. Peter was around at the time and all he did was criticise the boat. It was a hard, bitter criticism of the boat, which I felt was completely misplaced. He said that the balance wasn't right, the wood hadn't been planed properly, and it leaked. In short, it was a shit job. My grand presentation had been reduced to a simple, naively put together African product. The expedition dream was crushed.

A squadron of bats sped across the gloom. Was it time to bell the cat and tell him how I felt and thought? The tickling feeling along my skin, the goosebumps and the empty hollow in my stomach. The early beginnings of a crack in the relationship, a bond was giving way.

Like a bird waiting to catch the last afternoon sun, woozy and self-contained, I ran to the beach, ignoring the criticism. The evening was breathtaking, completely absorbing. A full-blown saga of emotions emerged as I ruffled with people from different countries, cultures, and languages. I explored my role as a woman, my ambitions and desires. All the rules around women, all the nameless rules for us, was I not allowed to design a boat, know the seas, learn and understand its dangers, was this specifically male territory and women undermined and ridiculed if they dared try and venture into this territory.

Peter remained steely-eyed as he criticised my first attempt to conquer the sea, love and embrace it, in adventurous travel.

Was this all to keep us in line, under control? What a price to pay, I thought. It costs us our joy and happiness, both ways, men and women alike. My emotions floated, my mind cutting deep. My mind was travelling, delving into the meaning of our lives.

My excluded life, the hollowness in my stomach now more apparent. I thought, "all these calm and sweet women, under control, myself included, were we simply stress-prone and subject to outbursts and sometimes violence, crying or blaming ourselves. Was this the price we had to pay? Our silence. I was keeping the pain inside, never talking about it.

Sometimes we were pinched under the table, not literally, but squeezed silently, in front of others. As you scream and shout, no one really understands your erratic, emotional behaviour. We blame ourselves, unable to describe what's going on, what's going on behind the scenes, what's going on inside.

The hope of sailing with a kindred spirit floated away. I should have rammed it down his throat, exactly what I thought, but what was the point. It would have destroyed his little ego, a man so unsure of himself, so full of complexes. He took pride in diminishing others.

Our hearts give way, us ladies. Hugs and kisses, a sunset, wine, music and love. The sand, the beach, sand oozing through my toes. The lake, its shimmer, the metallic, turquoise hue it had taken over. It's freshness, we loitered around, celebrated, God knows what, we celebrated, laughed, woozy and self-contained.

The pain of criticism was silenced for that night but tucked deeply, waiting for its moment to erupt.

12 NOVEMBER 2015

Affet's Child and the Clinic

The next day, early morning, Paul, the maintenance manager, my right-hand man, was down with stomach cramps. I was told that Isaac, who was in charge of the ponds, was going mad.

'He suffers from *ngulu*,' Bernard the chef said. *Ngulu* was known as spirit possession, 'the spirits have possessed him, taken over his mind.'

'Isaac drinks, so every time he goes off drinking, he suffers from *ngulu*. He's not supposed to drink,' Bernard continued.

Two days later, Isaac pitched up and said, 'Madam, I have malaria. I know it's malaria and I need some medicine.' He was confident that he had malaria. He was sweating at a high temperature, shaking and shivering.

I dug into my bag of medicines, not sure of what I was doing.

I found some Co-Arinate. I instructed him to take three tablets every twelve hours. A couple of days later, he was back in action.

'Your *muzungu* medicine is very good, Madam. It's powerful!'

Placebo or real, it worked. He was better and life appeared to be back to normal.

I questioned why they all called me *muzungu* when clearly, I was black.

'You have *muzungu* behaviour Madam. You're a *muzungu*,' they said.

After more inquiry, I discovered *muzungu* had become to mean someone with foreign western behaviour. They called Indians *mwenye* and Chinese, *ma Chinese*. I was *muzungu* and the word never stopped. All the children in the village referred to me as *muzungu* as well.

As for Paul, he had ulcers, stomach pains and malaria all at the same time. We rushed off to the clinic in the pelican. Unfortunately, we found Simon the male nurse also down with malaria. He had body pain all over and gave himself a malaria diagnosis. In his weakened state, he examined and tested Paul with the simple malaria kit they had in all the clinics. A needle prick into the finger, a small blood sample and the results were ready within a minute.

'No malaria!' He confirmed. 'This could simply be some stomach bacteria, there's cholera around.' Simon prescribed two antibiotics to destroy the bacteria and an anti-acid for the ulcers.

Of course, Paul forgot to tell the nurse that he was drunk the night before, so I insisted he told the truth.

'No, Madam, I know I have malaria,' he insisted.

'Ok.' The nurse gave up. Out came more tablets, Coartem, recommended by the World Health Organisation.

'It's the best.' Simon handed him more medication and three days later, Paul was back to work. Everyone, it seemed had malaria.

It didn't take long before I realised that most of the shaking and sweating, was in fact, malaria. The medication taken immediately solved the problem within three days, sometimes less, depending on the person and his health condition. The earlier the medication was taken the quicker recovery.

Night fell and the lake shimmered, the diamond, silvery grey, almost metallic impression of the lake as the sun fell over it, the sunset mild, clouded over, the solar plexus soothed.

When the night fell, and the lake had this metallic impression, Simon called, 'It's Affet's son!'

Affet was one of my general workers and the guide I used to take guests to Kalambo Falls.

'He's dying, Madam. We need to rush him to Mpulungu. The boy is plump and I can't find a vein to inject him. He'll have to be rushed to Mpulungu general hospital and be put on an emergency drip of Quinine.'

'Simon, it's late. The lakes are rough and all I have is my 40hp. All my engines are down. It's that black market fuel we've been buying. There's a terrible shortage of fuel, so we've been going over to Chipwa Tanzania and we suspect it's the containers that might have been used for oil as well or some sugary substance. The mercury engines are sensitive. All my 60hp engines are spitting some frothy white liquid, crystallising sugar. We were told the engines would have to be taken to Lusaka. I don't know what to do. I simply cannot take the risk.'

Mother, father, coxswain, the mechanic, Paul, sick in bed, twisting with stomach cramps, I had no rescue team in case anything went wrong on the water, I had to make a hard decision, it would have to be early tomorrow morning.

It was a difficult night. *What if the child died overnight?* I thought. It was a prayerful night. Then, early morning, at the crack of dawn, Affet banged on my door. I leapt out of bed, wide awake. 'The boat is ready, Madam. Thomas is here and I need K200 for the admission fee and some food money.'

They were off shortly afterwards. The child was soon on a quinine drip in Mpulungu and a few hours later, I was informed by two women that the child was out of danger, 'Thank you, Madam, thank you.' These were the moments that made my day, made my life worthwhile.

It was early morning, I went singing and ran down to the lake. The sailing boat had just come in. The fishermen came with Nile perch, mpamba and buka buka. Christmas was near and the lake was full of everyday fish. There was no shortage of fish, but very little was left for the commercial market.

'You can only have the Mpamba, the buka buka and kapenta is for home.'

The season had just begun, two weeks from now, they'd be plenty and I'd have the full selection. For now, I had to do with Nile perch.

I smiled and took a snap, the sails were so quaint. Mpamba, white bait, kapenta were thrown onto my jetty. The personalised service. The white egret perched on the deck—the resident pied kingfisher questioning the intruder.

I taught Bernard how to fillet the Nile perch. We made a beer batter and had a classical fish and chips for lunch, using Chinese cabbage for the salad. Lettuce was impossible to find and all my attempts to grow it had failed. Either the monkeys would get the newly growing seedlings, or if they survived beyond that point, the lake flies would nibble the leaves before you got to them.

The soils were poor, basically, we were living along a beach. The beach soil continued deep into the land and growing vegetables was impossible. I would have to try something different, innovative and look into alternative ways to have a vegetable garden. The conventional garden in beds did not work here.

By lunchtime, the lake began to change. The afternoon waves came in rough and wild. They broke and shuffled roughly as the rains started building up. Affet's son was safe in Mpulungu, I needn't worry. I tucked myself in bed and caught up on the hours lost during a sleepless, prayerful night. I curled in the comfort of my chalet and wrapped in a duvet. I floated and disappeared into my dream world.

I woke up in the morning wanting to define what I was doing. The lake was a sanctuary, an assurance of privacy, a scientific research centre with treasured patrons, clients and researchers of long-standing, well-known celebrities in their field of expertise. No attempts were made to entertain them. Instead, they entertained themselves in books, computers, diving, snorkelling, and research.

When the weather was fine, excursions could be taken to Kalambo Falls. We took pride in our isolation. A guest once wrote— A place of distinction, Kalambo Falls Lodge. I took pride in this. It was quiet and serene, we had exquisite food.

Sometimes we had early nights, other times, we indulged in cocktails, wine, champagne and good company.

The students who came were all focused and ambitious. They were pursuing bachelor of sciences, masters and PhD degrees. The students held ambitions to get somewhere in life, write, present and lecture. The competition was noticeable, often bordering on jealousy, towards the accomplished.

Other guests who came to visit, men of distinction, such as Lord Torrington, Kasanka Trust patron, the German ambassador, Andy Anderson, all had a wonderful time. I received recommendations through word of mouth and slowly the place began to fill up.

The first signs of the rains came in November, and fish was difficult to find during this period. We struggled to get any fish for the pot and had to resort to trips to the Mpulungu market to buy it. The price was often double what we paid for the fish from Tukulungu.

The heat builds up in November too, and the lake can get pretty rough, especially in the afternoons as the storm threatens, accompanied by lightning and distant sounds of thunder. Early mornings, however, could sometimes have perfect sailing weather, with clarity and visibility.

The birdlife is prolific throughout November, sometimes palm nut vultures, a rare species that can be spotted. It flies like a kite and can be mistaken for one. The first fire finches arrive, the red, brown and Jameson's fire finch. A baby now in flight.

A paradise fly catcher to enhance the beauty of the bird life here. A little robin perched on the branch outside my open bedroom. Then flocks of mannikins, the bronze mannikins and then a Heuglins robin chirping in the forest. All these creatures, it seemed were waiting for the mid-November storm, announcing that the rains were here.

It was on 20 November that the storm finally gave way. It poured heavily, and the rainy season was in full swing. An impressive flow of water streamed into my property, flowing over the rocks and onto the steps by the fish ponds, rippling cascades falling from the hilltop, down across the steps, and into the lake.

The next morning, the skies were crystal clear, the heat and the humidity disturbing. I ran to the ponds to watch the last of the running water. The dry stream was alive and running. The pond area flooded. I peeped my head into a pond to watch the tropheus dubois gaily swimming.

In the pond was a reflection of a circle and point with flashes of rainbow colours. I looked up to see what was creating this effect and in the sky was a massive circle surrounded by rainbow colours. I knew from this moment that I was protected and something special had to come out of this place; perhaps that is why I loved it so much.

A flock of red-winged starlings came to settle on the roof of my thatched dining area. The storms became the norm, and then the bliss that followed after. That night I went out in the evening, with my coxswain and his assistant. On the water were fishermen with hundreds of baby nkupi thrown into a small wooden boat. They were using mosquito nets to fish, and another boat was filled with the tiniest kapenta I had ever seen.

The whole thing was disturbing. I yelled and screamed at them but it had no effect. They laughed at me. I tried to explain the harmful effects of fishing using mosquito nets. They smiled and agreed but went on as soon as I departed. It disturbed me to see them destroy their future. Nkupi fetched such high prices at the market if they'd only give the little fish a chance to grow. As for kapenta, it was simply a question of controlling the size of the nets. No one cared and no one policed the villagers, so in effect, all they did was think of today, regardless of the repercussions for their children.

There was a full moon over the lake on 26 November. These are moments you never got enough of, a clear sky and the full moon rising from the forest behind the house. Sometimes I'd be up at 3 a.m. to watch the moon come down over the lake, moments I'll remember forever.

The whitebait had started to come in and was soon added to the menu. I tossed them in flour and fried them, sometimes in a light batter, another time dipped in a beaten egg, then rolled in flour and fried. The locals dried them a little, then fried them directly in oil and salted them afterwards. I tried different ways, making interesting sauces, mayonnaise with lemon juice, sweet and sour sauce, peanut butter dip until I could not look at whitebait anymore for the rest of the season.

Before the month drew to an end, my colony of monkeys returned to feast on the fig tree that had just come into fruit. The previous year it had come into fruit in October. This year it was November. I realised she really couldn't be relied on. She gave her fruit at different times of the year and every year could be different. When she did, the spectacle was magnificent. Monkeys, red-winged starlings, birds of all sorts sung and chirped to nature's bountiful generosity.

21 NOVEMBER 2015

Guests

It's strange when you have European guests, students, and large groups coming in the summer, their summer, our winter. A smaller group would continue monitoring their experiments and sometimes stayed till December.

As the host, I often wondered, *do I sit there and chat with the group?* Or do I serve them their meals and keep away? When you act the recluse, they invite you to the table and insist you eat with them. When you decline the offer, they assume you have complexes. When you sit with them regularly, they withdraw into their private thoughts, you become the fun spoiler, or they talk about experiments that go right above your head.

Peter, on the other hand, broke into easy banter. He talked a lot. He was up until midnight and up early morning with the students, eating breakfast, lunch and dinner with them.

One evening, I finally heard him say, 'You're not listening, listen.'

At this point, I took him to the side and said, 'What do you expect? Can you really buddy banter with people you hardly know, half your age? Sometimes guests want to be left alone. Please give them space.'

When Harry arrived as the new manager in the summer of 2015, it seemed natural. He was the age mate with many of the students. Some of the younger girls paraded around in the tiniest bikinis they could find, trying hard to get his attention. Others stared directly into his eyes. Harry was English, shy, with a stiff upper lip. He was the type of guy that women pounced on. He'd never make the first move. His excuse was, 'I'm the manager here.'

There were seventeen students in August, including Paul, Harry and myself. We were cooking for twenty people. My thoughts were a little muzzy, as my garden had just been over pruned and destroyed by Harry. The place was also in a mess. It was my little paradise, but my distress faded as I enjoyed what I did. By the fifth day, order had returned to the place. A system was in place and all went smoothly.

We cooked chicken, goat, duck and pig, all on open fires and slow cooks in a pot. The veggies were cabbage, rape, *kalembula* also known as sweet potato leaves and okra. Anything I could get locally, I used. It wasn't easy cooking here. There was so little in the market. It was almost impossible to keep a vegetable garden and the shops and butcheries in Mpulungu had very little that excited the kitchen or could inspire a chef. You learnt to cook with the basics.

We slowly learned to churn out hot pizzas, ciabatta, brown loaves of bread, savoury buns, pancakes, curries, fried rice, risottos, pasta and sauce. The secret ingredient was garlic. I bought kilogrammes of it from Shoprite Kasama. I carried dried herbs with me whenever I travelled. I was so used to cooking with fresh herbs in Lusaka that I quickly bought some old broken boats and stuffed them with leaves, sticks, and some manure from the village. I also brought in some decent soil from the forest nearby. I soon had fresh herbs— basil, mint, lemongrass, garlic chives, rosemary and oregano. The meals began to improve, and I was getting the taste right.

That gut feeling again. The slow coiling and clenching inside, the fiddling of fingers, the scratching of arms, why wasn't I getting this right. November was worse. Some stayed for more extended periods, some came back—that sick little slide in the guts. The strained smiles, strange silences, looking down or to nowhere. Lots of inner thought and reflection, grappling with words and strained conversation, ideas scattered here and there.

They were "kooky pals" amongst themselves, after all, and understood each other better. I wasn't sure at what informality to pitch myself at, this chattering group, they smudged it all over their faces, unable to drape it.

'We have so much to learn in this world,' the Serbian finally said, slowly getting to the crux of the matter. 'In Europe, we're so closed, we live in our boxed up world with blinkers. The more we travel, we realise there is just so much to learn.'

My thoughts ran off to the weird uneasiness in all our conversations, was it easier for foreigners to mingle with the poor, needy, uneducated African, where they feel they're teaching or bringing something new to the table or making a difference? Whereas with a black, like myself, educated, talented, strong, with as much exposure, education and travel, was it harder for them. Harder to comprehend, harder to grapple. Yet I had grown up less privileged but in a way, got to the same place. Suddenly, feelings of competition arise, comparisons, accomplishments, weighing themselves against you, it's something difficult to talk about, but egos meet and competition and comparisons the result.

I stared at the enormous wild fig that canopied my house and it felt like she embraced my thoughts, every night, my reflections and knew the guests' thoughts too.

One of the male lecturers, a PhD student grappling with emotions, feelings, and whatever was brewing inside, came with a charged sense of readiness. He vomited copiously, red-faced, his nervousness gave way, an uncontrolled attack, 'The ponds are not yet ready and they're leaking every single day. I've repeated it, there's nothing you've done. I'm leaving on the 26th and cannot complete my experiments!' He was screaming and shaking.

It was clear he was trying to find something wrong. Something to accuse me with. There was something deeper going on inside and the leaking ponds became his perfect ally. His outburst was completely out of order and clearly out of integrity.

I was prepared for this. I was waiting for something to erupt, the tension had taken its toll and the boil had burst. Calmly, I explained that we could continue to accuse each other but the best way was to find a solution, 'Let's all go together and assess the problem and find a solution together.'

The problem was sorted out in ten minutes. All the staff were tasked with repairing the leaks and assisting with the experiments. The experiments he was trying to sort out himself. A few hours later, he appeared with a deep apology.

At this point, I insisted on closer involvement in all experiments going on until summer next year when they'd all return. I chose to take charge, rise to the occasion and not allow myself to be 'shat' on. It was important not to get angry, and certainly, not to scream back.

I scrambled over the ponds, leaning over the tanks, studying the fish and enjoying their serenity and the speed they whisked from side to side, avoiding my hands. You really couldn't catch them. They were agile and smart.

The students needed their books, papers and research to make them somebody. I needed justification for my isolation on the lake, a library for research and a research centre. I had to remind myself that no one owes you your dreams, their friendship, their companionship, their time, their understanding and their explanations. We are in it for ourselves, so get on with what you want from this Vicky. Don't expect anything from anyone, especially not admiration or acknowledgement. You're in it for yourself.

This place was isolated, yet I loved it. Incidents like this came and went. It wasn't the first, it wasn't the last. People are people and relationships were hard work. Sometimes, even stressful. Physical stress I pleasured in, emotional stress was always harder to deal with.

My muzzy thoughts cleared, my focus, my eyes shifted to the shacks on the lakeside, the villages, their livelihood, the difference I made to them. An escape to a hospital in emergencies, an outlet to sell their produce. Employment, even if it was only part-time at times, somewhere to turn for extra cash.

Trips to Mpulungu were loaded with villagers jumping on the boat for a free ride. My presence was felt. It was a difference to their lives, and for me, I was enjoying the perfect isolation, the paradise, my Shangri La.

December 2015

In the first week of December, a little sailing boat arrived full of buka buka and Nile perch, the season's first catch. It was the beginning of the fishing season, guaranteeing that Christmas and New Year would be a bumper period for fish in the pot.

Along with the rains, the fish feast came, followed by snakes and scorpions. With their holes filled up and hiding spots disturbed, they were forced to search for alternative homes.

In the dining area, we killed about three snakes. Another day, a large, black scorpion was found in the toilet. I found a few in my little chalet. It felt like a scorpion invasion. In mid-December, we found a small, black spitting cobra in a student's suitcase. Thank God it was found in a zoology student's suitcase. She was more entertained and charmed by the little nuisance hiding in her bag than frightened.

When my family came over for Christmas, we spotted three green bush snakes. In addition, another small black spitting cobra found in the shower, a blind smooth-skinned black snake in the guest toilet, and an orange patterned snake we couldn't name. December was also the height of mosquitoes but worst of all were the midges that nibbled on everyone. You couldn't see them but everyone was covered in a rash of bites, scratching and itching. When they all left, I wondered if I'd ever see them for Christmas again.

JANUARY 2016

The Fig Tree

By January 2016, the fig tree had an abundance of fruit. I couldn't figure this tree out. The first year I arrived, she fruited in October, the previous year, it was December. Every twig filled with ripening fruit. The monkeys came home to feast, but this time the mothers held their little, newly born bundles to her waist. I realised they all gave birth at the same time.

At night the bush babies came out to feast on the figs. We spotted one in my lounge, another in the office and one just outside my house. What a noise they made at night, screeching and screaming like a crying baby.

There were kapenta fishermen everywhere, catching the smallest fry I'd ever seen. The nets were so small, and no one controlled them. I finally took it upon myself to report them to the police marine department, these murderers of baby fry. The police arrived at 7 p.m. to find the fishermen out with their paraffin lanterns. Within five minutes, all their lanterns went off. The city on the lake was in darkness. Mosquito nets were confiscated, and the group were lectured on good fishing practices. I felt so proud of myself.

Interestingly enough, instead of hating me, they all started to respect me. They smiled at me and listened when I chased them away from the beaches and breeding areas. I pushed them into deeper waters where fishing was allowed and did not interfere with the breeding. From then on, I started working with the authorities, plugging into the powers they feared and working alongside the headmen to sensitise the villagers that they were only ruining their futures and no one else.

January was when I noticed the dogs were full of ticks, not fleas. Big, black, bloody ticks. I soon found a veterinary shop in Mpulungu that sold seeds, fertilisers, animal dips, and other animal and farm products. It always amazed me the things you could find there, including dog dip. The dip was intended for cows and animal husbandry, but we used it for dogs and it worked well. It was also very cheap compared to all the vet bills I used to pay in Lusaka.

I had brought my three dogs, Gold, Harry Potter and Sunshine. Harry Potter was a pure breed miniature pincher. The other two mongrels were a miniature pincher and poodle mix, but they did look cute and were small enough to bundle up as I made my move.

My dogs loved the bush. They went crazy catching geckos, lizards and baby monitor lizards, which were plenty here. I watched as their hunting skills improved with time as they adapted to bush life and the wild. However, it irritated me when they trapped a creature, tortured it, and left it lifeless uneaten. Sometimes I was forced to relieve the creature of its pain and crushed its head.

The dogs tried their luck with the bush babies and monkeys but they were fast and far too intelligent. The bush babies slithered away like furry rats, the monkeys went crazy and called the others. They made such a racket while the mothers grabbed their babies and climbed the nearest tree, showing their teeth as they did so. This left my shrimp-like dogs completely dazzled, afraid and unsure of themselves. I finally understood why cats and dogs were not allowed in game reserves. They could be an utter nuisance, destroying the natural ecosystem and creating mischief.

Monkeys were not innocent either. I was nursing a small bird we had found running on the sand at Isanga Bay. It was a boiling hot day and the sand was burning. The little creature was frantic and didn't understand where it had run. My daughter and I caught it and took it home. The poor thing was so frail that we put it out on a patch of grass in the warm sun to gather strength. Within a minute, a monkey had spotted it. It came down the tree, grabbed the bird and munched its head off in a second. Once up and safe on the tree, it started plucking the feathers from the bird. It stared at us and wondered why we were surprised and angry at it. It continued to pluck the feathers slowly and ate the whole thing. *Such was nature, so cruel*, I thought.

December was also the month when you couldn't leave a jar of jam or honey open. Within a minute, bees descended on the jar. As this had become a frequent occurrence, I decided on bee boxes that I planned to set up in the forest behind my property.

I had also planned a deck. The views were so spectacular here that I brought in a foreman from Lusaka who was to help me construct a concrete deck where we could sit, sip some wine and contemplate while enjoying the serenity and peace of the lake. The sunsets were to die for. We needed more viewing areas.

By the end of January, the lake was still and calm. The rains were scattered and it seemed like a year of drought. Lusaka and southern Zambia were already experiencing shocking drought conditions. Here the rains were certainly less than normal and the reward for that was still waters. It felt like you were swimming in silk waters.

10 January 2016

Dear Georgie, Gay, Renuka, Temsy, Russell, Toby and Tim, (my friends in the UK who were following my life.)

It's 2016 and I wish you all a wonderful, prosperous and blessed New Year. I hope all your dreams come to fruition.

Zambia's going through unusual times, the kwacha falling, copper prices falling, the Chinese bubble festering and surely to burst one day. Africa will explode one day and collapse. We are far too dependent on the Chinese at the moment and it's frightening!

To add to all our sorrows looks like it will be another drought year. More power cuts follow this. I can't imagine that we're going to have a fruitful year as a nation. Here at the lake, we're cut off from the politics of the day, had I not been driven by some kind of determination, I would have given up long ago.

The challenges are immense. The logistics of getting something down here is a nightmare, enough to scare or chase anyone away. It is 1,000 km from Lusaka and when you finally get here, Mpulungu is gruelling hot. Although some of the stretch is picturesque and has some spectacular views, the last one-hour leg by boat before you get home, with sometimes wild and violent waves, can be your final blow. Sometimes I do feel, 'what the f.... am I doing here?'

Perhaps the price for paradise is high. The place begins to consume you. It grows on you strangely and mysteriously. Mpulungu town itself is an eyesore. Shabby African style stores are scattered and lined up everywhere you look—a filthy shoreline of marketeers and fishermen. Crates and boxes mangled in dirt and filth. Plastic, leaves, wood, boxes, tins and bottles. I guess it's Africa, what can I say? The mind does wonder as to what was and what could be.

Over Christmas and New Year, I had my whole family here, Gloria, Angelika, Michael, Tue, Eva, and Tue's mum. We went over to Kasaba Bay, now dilapidated but still has good memories of when that part of the lake was the Riviera of Zambia. We spent the night at Ndole bay, the only existing touristic destination remaining from colonial times. The area once had seven lodges in action, with people from all over the world visiting Lake Tanganyika from the Zambian side.

I met a lady there, reminiscing about Lake Tanganyika's good old grand days.

'An era gone, lost,' she sadly said. 'The potential of Mpulungu and its surrounding countryside, it's such a shame.'

I'm now well resigned to country life here and resigned to malaria that I get annually. I have a surplus supply of malaria medication, paracetamols, and general antibiotics for stomach cramps. I've become a nurse, doctor, cook, cleaner, tour guide and I guess I'm a tourist attraction as well.

In addition, I'm learning to speak Bemba with my i-school tablet. It is a wonderful application that teaches the Zambian primary school syllabus in the eight languages of Zambia, including English. So I switch from Bemba to English and it seems to be working. I'm slowly getting there. Unfortunately, everyone here speaks Lungu. It feels like trying to learn high German in Switzerland when everything you hear around you is dialect but your tablet speaks this perfect, deep Bemba. I insist on my high Bemba as it would seem a waste of time learning Lungu when it's so regionalised. I could use Bemba nationwide, and everyone here is forced to learn it at school anyway.

I'm now taking care of the ponds where scientific experiments are conducted. Not in my wildest dreams did I ever imagine that I'd be talking about the cichlids of Lake Tanganyika. Life for me has now taken on a new turn that I'd never dreamt of. A life I didn't know even existed. I had never heard of cichlids before.

It's wonderful working with young, highly intelligent and motivated people who are different from where I came from in terms of art, culture, theatre, basketry and literature. These are things I aspired to, all the easy stuff, I guess. I was never interested in science. Now I'm being forced to learn Latin names for all the fish, God help me. I'm learning about fossil-bearing sandstone layers, archaeological sites around Kalambo Falls, Moto museum housing all the research. It's fascinating.

I host researchers, spend evenings chatting, or smashing bottles of wine. Discussions range from bones, shaped stones, social organisation of cichlids, a lot of stuff is Chinese to me but I'm enjoying it all and soaking in what I can. Peter with his medical background, has found his niche. He soaks it and laps it all up. Peter loves it here.

He's now back in San Francisco, selling up, closing shop, in his words, "extinguishing all the flames," and hoping to be here, and making a life with me here on the lake.

It took me two years to finally rent out my house in Lusaka and make the final move. Without my daughter Gloria, who finally packed up my bags, knives, forks, glasses, sheets, paintings, sculptures, etc., I would have kept delaying the process. Not that I wasn't sure of wanting to move but because the work involved was so physically exhausting, I couldn't find the energy for it.

Gloria finally arrived in December 2015, with my home in boxes. She hired a truck and delivered every item worthy of keeping to Mpulungu. The last leg took us several trips, boat rides to and from Mpulungu to get everything down here. I now have all my belongings, finding a place for each item in my home. A little corner here, on a wall, places here and there. My stunning dining table, lounge suite and all are here.

I'm now in the process of putting up a 200 square metre deck to create a relaxed, easy area for my students. Unfortunately, my furniture created this formal, colonial ambience, which I don't quite think goes well with what I intend for the place. I would rather have it funkier and casual to accommodate the young and the academia.

I'm thinking of separating the two so that I'll have my gentlemen and ladies, like yourselves, and then keep an area that is more laissez-faire. The deck would be for the students, perhaps for the NGOs like Peace Corps and the likes, who frequently visit the place and prefer the more casual ambience.

I wish I could have the deck all ready by the end of the year, but as they say in Bemba, Swahili, and Lungu, "pole, pole," slowly, slowly. Life here is slow. No one understands speed and efficiency. The concepts do not exist,

I'm sure of it.

I'm learning to blend in with the people who indulge in the lake, all this seems to grow and deepen within me. I feel like it's all a splendid experience of soaking in the beauty. I'm also experimenting with the local cuisine and helping with the villages, schools, and clinics to make a difference. For now, I'm feeling my way through all this, wondering what my purpose here is, what will develop, what will come out of this. It's a life of reflection, I know, a turning point that will establish the last chapter of my life. I have no intention of moving from here, it's been so hard to get here. My only desire is to grow roots and reflect on life.

I love it here. Thank you, Toby for providing the foundation for my new existence.

All my love and blessings,
Vicky.

FEBRUARY - NOVEMBER 2016

Elections

February

By the middle of February, the clouds had gathered again to present us with a normal rainy season. The storms usually began at night. The lake started filling up rapidly, and we certainly were not experiencing a drought as they were in the country's southern parts. Every night a storm came and so did the floods. This year made it the third year of floods. Houses built close to the lakeside started to collapse. The winds were vicious, the rains wild and the storms shook the place.

'We've never seen storms like this, never before,' Happy the headman said, 'the storms are bringing us plenty of fish, nkupi, Nile perch and kapenta. We have a bumper year.' The fishermen were all smiling. They told me the storms had brought in the kapenta.

Sometimes I'd find the dining area full of water, damaging

my stunningly beautiful, Italian designed beechwood table. The table had been crafted by a genius in South Africa. The handcrafted table sat sixteen people. I noticed the first bubbles on the inlay. I worried about my pieces.

The students were also worried about their experiments in the lake and ponds. One massive storm and all the experiments in the lake came to an abrupt end. The cages lay mangled in the water somewhere. The one we retrieved was squashed.

A specialist called Heinz, an older, charming gentleman, was there with us. He often sailed alone, with his team from Mpulungu, diving at every bay, in his solitude, discovering the cichlids of the lake. He wrote about the fish and named some. Some of the fish were named after him. He loved the lake and returned every year for new discoveries. This time he was assisting the younger students and professors with their findings.

He was a chemist by profession, but cichlids were his personal hobby, collecting over 50 aquariums in his private collection placed in the basement of his home in Basel. Just to show, how so many people, silently, privately, were addicted to this lake, returning year after year to experience and take part in its mystery.

Besides the abundance of fish, the storm brought, wild mushrooms in the forest. The villagers came daily to sell all their fresh leaves, pumpkin leaves, sweet potato leaves and cassava greens.

By the end of the month, the last fish of the season was being smoked and dried. It was impossible to sleep with the smell coming from the lake. It was an unbearable, stinky smell.

I put my attention to the school in Chitili, knowing that this smell couldn't last long. There seemed to be so much work. It was impossible to decide where to start. I noticed there were no books, reading texts or reference materials. Children came to school with an exercise book and pencil. The teachers had a few manuals that they relied on. The board was the wall, partly painted with black. There were a few desks and chairs, which meant most children sat on the floor.

The sun came in over the hills one morning and reflected on the lake. Three families of black-spotted otters smoothly swam into the bay. I had never seen so many otters in a group and each family appeared to have a baby. I sat on the jetty, legs dangling over the edge. I noticed one of the otters had stealthily swum close to me and peeped out of the water to see my face. We were eye to eye. The otter gave me the warmest feeling.

As I walked back to the deck, I noticed that the trees were full of birds. The trees were filling up with homemakers. The garden looked fabulous, lush and green. The villagers had a bumper kapenta season. On the same day, a hippo and its calf appeared at the bay.

Happy rushed to announce that they had spotted a hippo and the villagers planned to kill it.

'It's a danger to us,' he said.

I tried to convince him to leave it as a tourist attraction. Hippos do give a warning sign if you get close to them, so I was sure that there was no problem if we just left it alone. We could live together. He wasn't going to hear of it, and a few days later, I heard that they had killed and distributed its meat among the villagers. Apparently, it was soft, tender, and delicious red meat.

What could I say? At some level, I was also happy that we could swim safely. This was the first hippo I had sighted, and that didn't last long either. It ended up in someone's stomach. If you wanted to see animals, you crossed the lake over to Nsumbu game reserve, where all the animals such as crocodiles, hippos, elephants and more were protected.

March

I received a call from the Office of the President that they were sending a delegation of twenty police and immigration officers for lunch. They wanted traditional food, so we prepared nshima, rice, fish, meat and vegetables.

The senior officers dished out first as the juniors waited for their turn. What surprised me was the amount they dished out. None of them seemed to respect that there were others to follow. Their plates were filled to the brim, and food fell off their plates. I panicked that I would not have enough food. I had no idea just how much one person could eat. We finally got to the last person, and there was enough to go around but only just. It was clear that if ever I had a delegation like that again, I'd dish out for them.

They cut the cake and placed the dessert on top of their meal. I had intended to serve coffee and cake afterwards but all in vain, the cake was eaten on top of the main meal.

It was a trying experience for me. I was sure that in the future, I would take more control, serve my guests, and be firm on respecting the others to follow, even if they were subordinates.

It wasn't right to allow the ones in authority to dish out so much with no regard for their juniors. It left a sour taste in my mouth. The way we undermined and disrespected what we thought were the junior officers, or the people under us, this sense of hierarchy and disrespect for our juniors, always irritated me.

April

April was here and the students arrived. That evening, some of the students went out to experience the lake at night. They decided to dip into the lake on their return but found the lake cloudy and impossible to get any vision. Investigations revealed that there were millions of jellyfish floating in the lake. This caused a cloud underwater. A few jellyfish were brought in for further investigation.

The fishermen explained to me that on days like this, you couldn't fish. They waited until the jellyfish moved on and that could take days. There was nothing they could do until the jellyfish disappeared. All that appeared underwater was a cloud; visibility was impossible.

May

The lake was at its highest in May. It hadn't been that full for a long time. Its highest water levels were last recorded in 1998. Martin at Waterfront started building a new bar because he noticed that the lake continued to rise every year. He didn't want to take any risks.

During the month of May, I discovered bottles of whiskey gone, a bottle of pink champagne I had kept for my birthday in July, missing. But that wasn't all, the company computer, my son, had bought me as a present had disappeared and some solar lights were gone too.

The company phone was gone as well. I called the police in and unfortunately, the evidence pointed to one of my staff members. A cleaner called Peter who was an amazing worker and expert snake handler. He could catch any snake and had no fear of the black mamba that we all feared.

He once saw a black mamba going into a hole close to one of the chalets. Peter grabbed its tail, pulled it out of its hiding place and crushed its head with one strike. It was over three metres long. I appreciated having him around. Reluctantly, I had to let him go as a statement to the rest. An example, I had zero tolerance for stealing.

June

Before I could catch my breath, winter arrived. There was no fish around even though June was the beginning of the fishing season. But this year, there was very little to no fish. The headman complained and, the fishermen were upset. No one could understand why there was no fish around. To me, it was clear that they had overfished. It was clear why there was no fish around, they used mosquito nets to fish, well it needed no explanation.

The worst of it was that they pulled the nets onto the beach, a practice called 'beaching.' This brought in all the breeding mothers who came to the shoreline to breed. Nothing could be more harmful to the lake and the fish than this practice. It had to be stopped.

July

The kapenta season was in full swing. Nile perch, nkupi and buka buka were difficult to come by, but the place was full of kapenta. The fishermen fished in the wrong places, too close to the mainland and breeding areas. So my next move was a trip to the fisheries department to see if we could get some floaters around to protect the breeding areas. It was a job I disliked, and it would take a lot of time to convince, may be costly. I could get the wrath of the villagers, but it seemed so urgent that someone had to take a stand to protect the breeding areas.

August

My cause seemed trivia, it was election time, and everyone was campaigning. Edgar Lungu for Patriotic Front (PF) became the man of the moment to continue running the country. He was elected on 20 January 2015 after Michael Sata died. Sata had died on 28 October, 2014 in London, United Kingdom. Lungu was completing Sata's term and was seeking a fresh term. It appeared to be the most violent elections I'd ever witnessed. There were lots of killings going on. I was in Kasama for two days, shopping, visiting Mwelwa Rock Art and Chishimba Falls. Everyone was talking about the elections and there certainly was fear.

I was happy to rush back home to my peace. The lake seemed to exist in its own reality. No one in Chitili really cared about politics. All they wanted was to benefit from the chitenge fabrics, bags of mealie meal, T-shirts and caps distributed. Of course, they would all vote for Lungu because he was the man that Michael Sata had chosen. They all loved Sata, the leader who had suddenly died in office, the man of the people.

Spring was here. The lake was calm and clear, perfect for snorkelling. The worst part of August was the bush fires that spread across the country. Where had this custom come from? Traditionally, it was to keep the snakes away and reduce ticks and fleas, but it seemed like the whole country had gone mad. Every natural forest was up in flames. It broke my heart, and the government did nothing about it.

In Tukulungu, I felt the impact first-hand. The lush green grass turned gold in June, July, it was stunning. It looked like a sea, a field of golden wheat. Overnight this golden field was burnt. It turned black, with ash, smoke and a grey cloud in the atmosphere. This disaster lasted the whole of August, right up to November, when the rains began. The natural flora and fauna all in flames. We missed out on the beauty of spring, where we would celebrate and enjoy all the autumn colours of our spring, 'the flush,' it's called. The grass goes gold, and the leaves turn yellow, orange and red. All this is lost because of this stupid, ridiculous custom of burning the grass.

So much more is lost. Creatures, birds, animals were killed in this blaze. We destroy a forest that is home to mushrooms, mopani worms, flying ants, honey, nutrition for millions in rural areas. It's just a question of time. If we continue this practice of burning, all this will disappear one day, it's only a question of time.

11 August was Zambia's election. I was more interested in a striped field mouse I had spotted, the first I'd ever seen. The staff went to vote. I didn't. I was not convinced that Sata's choice of man was the answer for the country. He won the compassionate vote, voted in because Sata had chosen him. To honour the man they loved, Michael Chilufya Sata, the majority voted Lungu in.

I was not convinced that he could make any difference to the country. I'd learnt from African politics that the choice of successor was always a sycophant, a yes-man and never the one with leadership qualities. The actual would-be successors, the men with vision, were often persecuted or dead. A president's choice of successor in Africa was undoubtedly a weakling, someone he could bully around, someone he could mould, someone who was 'user-friendly.'

When the researchers arrived, they found lots of jellyfish around. This time someone came whose interest was jellyfish.

The ambience was magnificent, with the research team around. For the first time, we had a worm expert.

September

I had a small group of lecturers who had stayed on. I was outside picking flowers for the table when I noticed that the sky was strangely dark, cast over. I ran up to the professionals asking them to come and explain to me what was going on. The lecturers were delighted and immediately identified it as an eclipse. They took out a few homemade gadgets that reflected what was happening on a piece of paper. It turned out to be an eclipse of the sun. There would not be another one for another 200 years. It was such a magnificent feeling to be the one who had noticed that something special was in the air.

That week, we watched baboons come in to drink water, another rare sighting. One of the lecturers who had been frequenting the lake for over thirty years told me that the trip into Kalambo River was full of baboons playing on the cliffs in the early days. However, year after year, their numbers reduced due to poaching.

What remained was the last colony of no more than eight baboons that found their refuge and safety close to us. I started to see them more regularly at the back of the lodge in the small forest I protected. They felt safe close to us.

During the eclipse period, I tried my first dive with the kindest and most professional diving instructor and researcher. He told me I was a natural. I remembered the last few minutes, suddenly being afraid of suffocating and briskly came to the top.

It was an experience of a lifetime, underwater, meditating, contemplating, one with nature, in harmony, one with the world of peace, calm, still, harmony is the word. It's a hobby I want to pursue.

By the time the researchers left, the leaves in the forest had begun to change, from green to red, yellow, orange, all the colours associated with autumn. This was our spring.

I drove to Lusaka to catch a flight to France. I wanted to be there for the rest of September to experience the Feast of St. Michael, which took place the last Saturday of September.

I spent a month at The Bonfin, the spiritual retreat I spend year after year going back to. I go there to experience that oneness with God. It's a long journey, a path to enlightenment.

A path I had embarked on from the age of eighteen years old. It's a journey that never ends. Regardless of the time, it would take. Lifetime after lifetime. Coming and going. Perfection, oneness with God, back to the bosom of the Creator, our long term goal. This would take centuries, lifetimes here on earth. Through pain and suffering, we acquired wisdom. Wisdom, our reward, and then one day, bliss. Finally, back to the bosom of our creator. That was our long term goal.

October

I had spent September in France. I missed the leaves changing colours. The heat built up in October. The lake was at its lowest this year, the fig tree refused to fruit in October, and there was no symphony of birds. The unusual breaking of the skies and the first rains appeared on 1 October.

A large nkupi was brought in, and I froze it immediately. I planned to prepare it for my son, Michael. Peter was going to Lusaka and I wanted him to deliver it to him.

Our darling Percy, my golden Nile perch, had developed some black spots on his ferns and lips. Initially, I thought it was some dirt, an infection, or parasite, but Isaac, who had been trained by Toby, confirmed that it's something they had noticed every year. It seemed to last for a month, and then it disappeared. All I could imagine was that this poor little darling, male or female, was sexing. Had he been in the wild, that's probably the colours he'd adapt to attract a partner or was he trying to camouflage against predators? Not even the professionals, the researchers, the academics, the lecturers could explain the unusual situation. We all assumed he was sexing. No one was sure. Not enough research had been conducted on the golden Nile perch. As for his age, we could only guess about thirty years.

November

With kapenta season out of the way, the reward was nkupi coming in daily. I had researchers around, so together, we spotted a woodpecker, a cardinal woodpecker, I was corrected. I loved having professionals around, so I opted to take them to Ungingi Pans in Mbala, where we watched some yellow-billed stock.

November always brought with it the rains, and my house was collapsing. The lounge and dining areas were leaking. The thatcher had done such a bad job that one year later, the lounge and dining area was a pool of water. The floor had started to give way, both the foundations of the dining and lounge had slowly started to sink, a disaster in the waiting. The lounge was the worst, and after a few storms, it dropped a few centimetres. The only solution was to break it down, smash a big hole in the lounge area and recreate a new floor. It needed to be reinforced with steel and solid concrete.

By 9 November, Peter and I were sitting in the dining area, using this space for everything we did. The lounge was forbidden territory, except for the builders repairing the floor. We brought the television from the lounge area into the dining to watch the American election. Peter was up all night, glued to the television, and disturbed by what was going on.

'Don't worry, who'll ever vote for an idiot like Trump? By morning, we'll be popping champagne. Good night, see you in the morning,' I said.

When I woke up for a coffee in the morning, Peter was in a state. Trump was in the lead and winning. I was shocked, unable to believe what I was hearing.

'Oh my God, what's this world about? Where are we heading?' I was breathless, gutted and wondering if I'd ever understood America and the American people. To vote for Trump, what did this say about the people? Over fifty per cent wanted a man like that, in my mind, an idiot, trouble causer and megalomaniac.

The man talked without thinking. He was racist, anti-African, anti-Chinese, believing in the supremacy of the white race. People like Trump would only accelerate this dreaded future of yet again, another Third World War. That was my fear around Trump and perhaps Peter's too and others for that matter.

I rushed for my first coffee of the day as I attempted to comprehend and perhaps dilute what I'd just heard. I noticed from the kitchen window the newly born baby fire finches, cutely pecking at Matata, my dog's leftovers of nshima and kapenta. Nshima and kapenta were his staple diet, besides his dog pellets that I brought in from Lusaka.

December

It was 8 December when I got a surprise call from my brother Noble Findlay. He is the oldest son in our family of thirteen and the founder member and managing director of Autoworld. He was in Mpulungu and planned to give me a surprise visit. We were charmed. I got Thomas to get the boat ready and swiftly pick him up from Waterfront. Joyce and Martin's pub at the waterfront, called 'Waterfront,' had become our favourite joint. We picked up our clients from there, landed the boats there and loaded from the Waterfront. I also stored my goods there when we couldn't cross.

Noble spent a few days with us. I was out of sorts and vomiting from a bout of malaria, so I wasn't good company at all. Peter took over and took him fishing. My staff prepared him meals. I felt awful that I couldn't be a good hostess. I spent the three days in bed recovering. What I do remember, however, it was what he said, 'This is my biggest regret that I didn't buy a place on Lake Tanganyika. Now I'm too old and sick.' He now had a heart problem. 'You're living my dream, Vicky.'

I knew and was convinced that I was living many people's dream: A life in the sun, a beach resort, fishing, swimming, snorkelling, diving, working with researchers, students, cooking and creating magnificent meals. My life was a dream, a fantasy and I had to recognise this. My life was perfect!

Martin, at Waterfront, was a reservoir of factual information about the lake. I wondered why he hadn't written a book yet. He had spent 40 years on the lake and was an authority in Mpulungu. I enjoyed our conversations, and while we discussed the old days and planned the future, Joyce ran around inspecting the place. She checked the books, took stock of the inventory, and ensured the place was clean. Joyce was a hard worker, solid, grounded and perfectly suited for Martin.

'Everything I'm doing here is for Joyce. She's much younger

than me, and if I go tomorrow, I have to be sure that Joyce won't struggle. She'll have all this, so she's got to learn to maintain it. I don't know how much longer I have, but I've no intention of leaving my family struggling. She'll be fine. She's a hard worker, and everything here is for Joyce.'

I remember repeating this to some of my staff, we were at Waterfront, waiting to cross, and I explained to them what this *muzungu* had told me. They were surprised that a man could leave everything to his wife and worked hard to ensure that she didn't suffer if ever he were taken away before her.

The initial surprise was replaced by admiration and respect. I understood it later as something that rarely happened in the village setting. If a man died, his relatives would come and claim all the wealth. The widow was generally left penniless unless she ran to victim support services at the nearest police station.

Once a man died, his wife was lucky if she had children, especially sons who could take up the responsibility of taking care of her. A son's wealth was shared between his wife and his mother. Often women lost their homes, furniture, money, and everything else.

There is often drama in the villages. I once took it upon myself to fight for a woman who had insulted her son-in-law because he mistreated her daughter. He beat her daughter and wouldn't stop. Doris worried he'd kill her. Powerless, she began to insult him in an attempt to stop him from mistreating her daughter further. She went to the extent of making reference to his penis.

'*Chikalachowe*!' she blurted out.

Her son-in-law immediately reported his mother-in-law to the headman. She was summoned by the headmen and punished. Her punishment was to compensate her son-in-law with money, a goat and a few other items. She was utterly devastated. Her attempts to apologise and explain herself yielded no results. Everyone waited for the compensation.

She came to me and begged for money. I was enraged by this and called in the headman for some explanation. I threatened him that I would go to victim support and bring in the police if they continued to treat women this way. Further, I would stop helping them with the school and buying their river sand and stones.

I think it's the threat to cut them out of business that worked, but I was warned that it was not my place to interfere in their customs and traditions. I had to stay out of village politics.

'Do we interfere in your business, Madam? Please, do not interfere in our village affairs,' the headman reprimanded me.

I accepted but firmly told them that all business would then go to Chitili village. I think I did win that battle, and Doris was forgiven on this occasion. However, I'm not sure how she suffered in other ways after that because she often came to complain about how difficult things were. I soon realised that if you gave a finger, they wanted a hand. Every gesture I freely gave was followed by a troupe of others begging. I disempowered the person I gave to and perpetuated their begging. I soon learnt not to be too free in my giving. Unfortunately, even the friendship offered was taken as a passport to beg and ask for things. It forced me to withdraw and insist that I paid for services or produce.

THE YEAR 2016

I'd got myself so busy, I had less time to write and read. My life was a constant play of musical chairs, running from Mpulungu, Chinsali, Lusaka, and then there was Kafue, my bushman's camping site, on the Kafue River, to take care of, as well. I felt split in all directions. Putting things together and letting go of stuff proved much more difficult than imagined. Added to all my problems was the constant menace of my car, which kept breaking down.

I was in the middle of a painful legal battle with Charles Davy, who'd lied to me, and together with his lawyer, Andrew Howard, formed a conspiracy to fraud me, and indeed they did, financial fraud, it was called.

I was a 100 per cent shareholder of my farm, Le Soleil, now Roma Park. I put together a complete business plan with diagrams, plans for houses, engineering designs and all. I had the whole project ready to go. All I needed was an investor to inject the required money, US$ 40 million.

The project was in the hands of several investors but Mr Davy was the first to claim that he would bring in US$ 48 million, he would become the majority shareholder and I would take on twenty per cent.

My contribution was the land and the project itself. His was the money and the expertise. It all made sense to me, rather be a twenty per cent shareholder of a large project than a hundred per cent shareholder of something you have no money to develop.

It all sounded great. As the project went forward, things started to change, as all crooks do. The US$ 48 million they promised to bring in was all one big lie. Instead, they started selling my land to raise the capital they needed for the project.

Slowly I found myself being pushed out. Further, I was never supposed to pay for infrastructure roll-out. My contribution was the land and the project itself. Together with the help of their crooked lawyer, they changed the contract, and in the new contract I signed, I had been hoodwinked, now I had to pay for infrastructure roll-out. Of course, I didn't have this money, and here the problems started.

I was born tough, ready to fight for any woman's cause, so I wasn't going to let Mr Davy or any white man think they could easily hoodwink me. I took the matter to the courts.

I'd hoped that by moving to the lake, I could divorce myself from the stress of legal matters, but it only exasperated the situation. I was constantly on the road, forced to drive to Lusaka to appear in court. The stress began to weigh me down. I found it hard to enjoy my paradise. I was on the road or going through sleepless nights, going through the case, the fraud, the deceit, the lies.

All I wanted was silence, peace and serenity. I liked being alone and loved my own company. I needed my space, my Shangri La.

Driving long distances alone, my mind would float. The cruelty of this world, the lies, the deceit, the greed, the jealousy, the competition. Sometimes my mind would quickly shift to the intelligence behind the organisation of this world.

Could witless, stupid, chaotic chance have organised this world? I questioned. This world was so intelligently organised. The harmony of the stars, the cosmos, the universe, it's precision and organisation. How could anyone possibly believe in the absurd or blind chance? Could atoms combine by chance? Could brains endowed with intelligence be left to chance!

Had I got myself into this mess by chance? No, I had to take responsibility and take the lesson given, learn my mistakes, address my naivety my over-trusting nature. I needed vigilance to be vigilant. It's what we were taught at church, be vigilant, my child. Why didn't I learn to understand the importance of vigilance?

I wasn't in the best place and could feel my nerves breaking inside me, the stress of the court case and the differences with Peter. His smoking got worse, and I could feel us drifting apart.

The court case got more intense. There were more demands from the lawyer, always monetary, of course. I could feel the stress getting the better of me. To add to my worries, I then received a call from my ex-husband, something that never happened. He passed the phone to my brother, a family I no longer saw. I had gone my own way. It sounded like a voice from another lifetime, a voice so distant.

I had found comfort in a more spiritual existence. I did not think about money anymore. My paradise taught me this. I loved it so much. I despised the times I travelled to Lusaka for court dates or visits to my lawyer for more information.

The call said something like, 'Your son's a mad man! In fact, he belongs in Chainama. So you'd better come down and collect him or take him to Chainama.'

Composed, I replied, 'Thank you, I'll see to it.' I muted the phone. If I wasn't already overloaded with pain and confusion, the news was the nail in the coffin. This call was my final goodbye to my ex and to my family. The insensitivity of the call shocked me.

I drove to Lusaka and insisted that Michael come home and spend some time with Peter and I, as it was close to Christmas. I could sense his agitation. He was rough, intolerant, nervous, impatient, but he agreed to drive down with me. Peter had a medical background, and fortunately, Michael got on with him. We needed time together to assess the situation and act from there. He came for Christmas, which we spent in Tanzania, and he left.

MICHAEL, JANUARY - APRIL 2017

January 2017

I had guests over from Denmark. Jesper and his family were here, keen to assist with the school's affairs and the clinic. They were here with me till New Year's Eve. However, my mind was on Michael. All I wanted to do was jump in my car and go see my son.

He had gravitated to a bunch of gregarious friends. Their eyes beaming and loud, he had been jolted out of his pensiveness. The child I knew was quiet and pensive. It appeared to me he was playing, acting the part, trying to fit in with his new friends. In reality, he was unable to keep up with the pretence. He was shrinking, like a hedgehog, curling up like a *chongololo*, the millipede, rolling itself into a curled tight roll, in self-protection. Unfortunately, at the same time, cutting himself from joy and self-expression.

He was confronted with exuberance, inspired by his newfound friends, who were loud and gregarious.

He poured out his emotions to me, sometimes violently, angry at me, other times tearfully, simply not coping. He felt his mind was being taken away from him, his talents stolen. He was losing himself. His sense of perfection was not there anymore. He thought he had studied too much, spent his life getting top grades and hadn't opened himself to the lightness of life. He was full of 'issues,' he described himself.

His friends were rollicking party animals. They plunged into a conversation. They had rowdy fun. They were outgoing and confident, so it seemed. He was passive, obedient, a victim of male power, his father and father's friends.

He became warmly defiant, prattling on fervently, self-assured but in a megalomaniac stupor. Inside, he was pretentiously self-assured, emotionally destroyed by the mental and verbal abuse by the male chauvinists he aspired to, wanted to be, or imagined he could be.

For Christmas, we decided on a trip to Tanzania. Unfortunately, the holiday in Tanzania was painful. It was clear I was losing my son. There were violent attacks, obnoxious behaviour, inconsistent outbreaks followed by gentle, loving-kindness.

I needed help. We both needed help. I returned to Lusaka with him and immediately approached a psychiatrist. The psychiatrist asked me ten questions to which I replied yes to all.

The diagnosis was simple. 'Your son has bipolar.'

His situation was critical. He'd become a danger to himself and others. He became megalomaniac, arrogant and verbally abusive with the potential to physically hurt himself and others.

We decided to medicate him secretly. 'It will take him about three to five months to calm down. After that, you will have your son back, don't worry. The medication will bring him down to an even keel. It's a chemical imbalance in the brain. However, the danger is he could kill himself. I've had clients who think they can fly. Some imagine themselves to be Superman, Spider-Man and throw themselves off balconies.

Others get arrested and end up in institutions. The easiest way was to medicate him discretely. Once he's settled and becomes easy to talk to, we can then sit down with him and discuss his situation and then work out what his future life could be. For now, what we need to do is to normalise the situation.' This was the psychiatrist's advice and it sounded right. What can you do with someone who is ranting and raving?

It didn't take long, I hung around in Lusaka and by March, Michael's situation had drastically improved. The medication made him sleepy, he was home often and I cooked him his favourite meals, Thai curries with coconut milk, ginger, garlic, lemongrass and lemon leaves soaked in the sauce.

We started laughing and joking again, it was wonderful. The moments I spent with Michael were so precious, and I felt my baby coming back. His gentleness returned, but his talents, memory and sharp intellect faded.

Once April had fallen, I felt immersed in the most challenging time of my life. The Davy case continued, but a sense of relief sprung as someone from the team approached me to talk about an out of court settlement. There was a lot of comfort in this, I felt I was finally getting them to bend a little, not that they offered anything exciting, just a little ice cream to lick while they screwed you up.

It was clear, I'd got to them, and they were concerned. People like that, I thought, needed to be nailed to the cross or pushed into a corner until they couldn't breathe. That's the only way you actually deal with people of that disposition who are insensitive to the sufferings of others. I was a woman on my own, taking care of three children. Where was their compassion?

I decided to return home, relieved; Michael looked better and handsome as usual, the scary, fiery eyes had disappeared and the gentle soul had returned. Just before driving back to the north, I was approached by an American who offered me the opportunity to look for sites in the rural areas along the main roads, they wanted to open up shopping malls nationwide.

I felt excited once again to be on the road driving through Kapiri Mposhi, Serenje, Mpika, Chinsali and Kasama. I spent a night in each town, assessing the areas for potential shopping mall sites. Five days later, I was back in Mpulungu, the answer to my tropical island, my seaside dream, I was home. I realised just how the lake had blessed me by fulfilling so many of my fantasies. Here there was nothing, no decent hotels, no large resorts, only simple bungalows and chalets.

We lived amongst nature and in harmony with it. I lived an eco-friendly existence, with waters that were breathe-mint clear, emerald green, turquoise, sometimes blue. It's a hard place to leave. Strange things happen to you here, and strange things happen to time. You lose your sense of time. I know that I kept growing roots here. I was taken in by this thirst that I simply couldn't quench.

I spent hours just watching the birds weave their nests, in and out of the trees and shrubs, monkeys stealing what they could and curiously watching my eyes to assess how far they could go and how much more they could steal without being noticed.

I was back at the lake, and life got back to normal. It was the first of April. I called Michael to tell him that President Edgar Lungu had banned nightclubs and discos, knowing that was the love of his life at the time. Of course, he fell for it, but I couldn't keep the joke for long. Finally, I laughed because of his reaction of shock, anger, disgust, 'shit!' That's all he could express.

I tried another joke with the girls: Lungu had banned mini skirts and women going into hotels unaccompanied by a man. But, knowing my sense of humour, they were far too smart, 'Good try, mummy,' they said.

'Shit,' I responded, 'doesn't seem to work with you girls.' We giggled over Michael's reaction.

My garden was a living jungle, the vegetable garden laden with herbs going wild and unused. Everything around was lush, green, full and wild. I was away, but all of it was splendid, the deck slowly, crawling along, *panono*. It wasn't my priority anymore; Michael became my centre of attention.

11 April 2017

The moon was full. All I longed for was that early morning when the moon fell over the lake, kissing her good morning. What a spectacular sensation! The rains were ending, and all the staff were sick, down with malaria. I understood this as a pattern, November, December when the rains began; everyone was down with malaria. It seemed to be a pattern that repeated itself as the rains ended. Obviously, the stagnant waters became the breeding places for the deadly parasite.

Peter was away in Mpulungu for two days. He planned to use the time to complete our website. The reception in Tukulungu was so poor it was impossible to create the page. He stayed at Charity's place, Nkupi Lodge and hoped to get better reception to complete the job.

I enjoyed my time with Charity at Nkupi Lodge. If I needed any gossip about who's who in Mpulungu, it was Charity, I asked. She had been running Nkupi Lodge for over 20 years now, and there was no one she didn't know and somehow knew their secrets too, much of which we kept to ourselves and laughed. She became my gossip partner.

My cash was low. I was constantly battling with Mr Davy, fighting for my dividends and shares in Roma Park. It was a nightmare but I wasn't going to worry about it.

The lake was calm and clear but there were very few fish around, and the cichlids were scarce. So it was not the best time for snorkelling.

A few days later, I went to pick up Peter and decided to continue the trip to Kasama to show him the Chishimba Falls, a masterpiece of three waterfalls in one. On the way, we visited the most outstanding fish farming project I had ever seen, and it was undoubtedly a model for Zambia. It was owned by an Iranian couple whose son, Sameen, happened to be Michael's friend. The couple were both engineers and settled in Kasama. They set up a highly sophisticated and engineered fish farming project, of Lake Tanganyika bream. They also had a sugar cane plantation and produced Kasama sugar.

Their home was impeccable, stylish, modern and overlooked

a man-made dam. I wondered why people chose to live in the city when there was so much beauty and potential in the rural areas. The family's home was illustrative of this.

Peter had been thinking of fish farming in the lake but after the visit, it was clear that fish farming required a considerable investment, know-how, and a strong scientific side as well. I certainly had lost interest in pursuing the fish farming project, on the other hand, the idea of producing fingerlings, which was less complicated, still lingered. Although we did have a set up of ponds that Toby had left, the question remained, what would we do with all the ponds? The obvious answer was the fingerlings.

By mid-April, the sky was blue, the winds were there, sometimes in the mornings, other times afternoons and often at night. Then, the clouds slowly shifted away, autumn arrived, and winter showed its face.

The poinsettias, acacias, flame trees were in full bloom in Mpulungu, the furry red grasses were out in full show and the fig refused to fruit that April. I guessed she needed a break to recuperate. In her place, the mulberries started to fruit. Unfortunately, they are a favourite of the monkeys. They never reached full fruition. The little brats munched them all as soon as they began to ripen, at the same time destroying the soft, gentle branches hanging over my nursery where I'd just put in lettuce and herb seeds.

The herb garden had finally taken off. I had basil, coriander, dill, garlic, chives, lemongrass, mustard leaves, mint and radish. The only way I could get some sort of a vegetable garden was to dig deep holes, then fill them up with dead leaves, bits of chopped up dried sticks and burned dumps of garbage. Once the holes were filled, we topped the beds with manure that I bought from the village. A mixture of goat and chicken droppings created a wonderful, organic heap; unfortunately, we had the vervet monkeys to contend with. The only things that survived were chillies and strongly flavoured herbs like mint, basil, garlic chives, lemongrass, mustard leaves and radish. Anything like rape, spinach, lettuce, carrots, beetroot, berries, guavas, mangoes, paw-paws, avocados ended up in their digestive systems. So I soon gave up on my vegetables and fruit and focused on chillies and herbs. In some old boats I'd bought from the villages, I did the same organic mixture and planted turmeric and flowers for my dining table, added thyme, rosemary and oregano.

I had been informed that Choppies, a Botswana supermarket chain was keen to move into northern Zambia. I was asked to see if I could find them ideal spots. It was an exciting time. Peter was away in Mpulungu working on the website, I was alone at the lodge, and for a long time, I'd been meaning to write a short history of my family. The Findlay family, a hundred years of Zambian history through the eyes of ordinary people and how the politics affected our daily lives, penetrating and corrupting our morals, principles, and very being. I started putting together my notes, calling it 'The Beautiful Ones Are Born,' an optimistic perspective hoping that new ones were born to change things.

I gathered the staff together for a short meeting and explained that we intended to embark on a new project, the production of fingerlings. The idea was to fill up the ponds bring that section of the business back to life, which would create more employment for the people, and perhaps an additional income that we desperately needed. The staff were all excited and eager to start the necessary work required. First, they prepared the ponds, which had cracked and required urgent repair. Again, there was excitement in the air and enthusiasm from all of us to nourish the project.

Peter returned with Rolf Shelton, the 'guru' of sustainable farming, reforestation and alternative economic lifestyles for the villagers and marginalised. Rolf had ideas around the forest, dried mushrooms, honey, drying green leaves, all alternatives to fishing, which was dying out as the primary source of income for villages on the lake.

'We have to look at green not blue money,' he said. It all sounded marvellous.

Living in Africa, I'd seen so many of these projects from NGOs and small scale industries. They all worked pretty well when the European or donor was around, but as soon as they left, the project fell to pieces.

Things got stolen and machines broke down that were never repaired, but I wasn't going to get this in my way. I invited all the villages and their representatives to participate in our first training programme on honey production that Rolf was going to organise.

I sensed Peter withdrawing as the excitement built up. Finally, Rolf said, 'I've never seen a man less interested in anything. I think he wants to do his own thing, and I can't see him getting involved in any of this.'

It was written all over Peter's face; on the contrary, I beamed with a passion for starting something that I felt the villages could benefit from—building honey boxes, placing them in the Lungu Forest Reserve above us, then waiting for the bees to do their job. I could buy and package the honey and deliver it to Lusaka. It seemed simple enough and I was eager to get going.

What I didn't know at the time is that Peter had already started looking for a piece of land of his own, around the corner from me, in an attempt to start his own project growing Moringa and curative plants. In addition, he planned to create a brand of alternative and natural products of his own. After all, he did have a medical and pharmaceutical background; therefore, creating the brand was up his street. *But why in the hell would you want to do that behind your partner's back?* Included in his plan were products such as honey and honey production. From that point on, he started visiting and contacting Rolf independently, without my knowledge.

I held my first training programme, beekeeping, inviting Morkell and Yolande from Isanga Bay to use the trainer. They could also train members of their staff and the villages closer to them in beekeeping. We all took advantage of the trainer I brought in from Lusaka.

May 2017

In early May, I travelled to Chinsali, and on my way to Lusaka, the road was lined with my favourite furry red grasses and yellow daisies. It was gorgeous, I loved this time of year. Long distant driving had become my time to think and reflect. All I wanted was silence.

Peter was left to take care of the lodge. Two weeks away, Peter and the staff had killed two black mambas found nesting in the kitchen roof. The larger mamba, which they took to be male, was about three and a half meters long, the female, they presumed, about three metres. These were monsters and presumably had been there for years. Black mambas could stay in one place for years as long as there was enough food around, mice, rats, lizards, geckos, frogs, or snails. These creatures were plenty at the lodge. Moreover, they hunted at night, so perhaps they might have come into the kitchen often or the courtyard where there was no shortage of something to eat.

Unfortunately, a few months earlier, I had brought in a cat to take care of the rats in the kitchen. What I imagined happened, the cat quickly cleared up the rats, much to my pleasure, but leaving the two snakes in my kitchen roof deprived of their accustomed dinner.

Thank God, I never ventured out at night for a cup of tea or midnight snack, which I'd always done living in a normal home. I brought it to an abrupt end when I moved here; just the thought of walking out at night to the kitchen was frightening enough, knowing that wild animals hunted best at night. I chose to sleep through the night, taking only bottled water with me.

After this incident, I chose to follow my instincts even more closely. For example, I might have been in the kitchen snooping for something to eat at the same time my dear friend in the roof would have chosen to sneak out.

A mamba in such a situation would feel trapped and threatened. My little Gold, a mix between a white poodle and a miniature pincher, had gone for a black mamba, like all my little 'munchkins,' attempting to protect me. I wasn't there at the time, but Peter told me that the mamba had gone straight towards my chalet, and Gold had gone straight for it. It wasn't even three minutes, and the dog died a paralytic death. I was so grateful I wasn't around to watch it.

When I returned, I was told that a crocodile attacked the two male ducks that swam in the jetty. One had disappeared, leaving blood spread all over the water. A crocodile was suspected to be around. Two days later, we heard that the villagers had killed a crocodile. We assumed it was the same one. This brought a sense of peace back to where the crocodile was caught. It had been mambas a week ago, a crocodile today, and that evening, one of the staff came running to say that he had spotted two hippos not far from us, going in the direction of the staff canteen.

The next day, another black mamba was spotted. It disappeared in the rocks near one of the chalets. For the first time in my life, I considered getting a revolver. It felt like something harsh, dangerous, and scary had invaded our paradise.

The staff were panicking. They had never seen anything like this before, three mambas within a month, two hippos, one croc, a duck taken, a dog killed, the whole place got this air of fear and dread, an eerie, spooky spell.

It was the end of May, the third mamba was never found, but by then, we'd stopped worrying about it. Peter Nyoni, the bee instructor, arrived to start the beekeeping training. The villagers had to choose their representatives to join the course, which we provided free. I paid for Peter Nyoni's expenses.

On the first day, twelve villagers attended. Peter had the art of teaching, and it surprised me how he kept the villagers' attention. They listened to him with excitement and enthusiasm. I rushed off to Mpulungu to collect the planks needed for the bee boxes. In the evening, we chatted about all the by-products we could eventually produce as well, honey mead, royal jelly, nougat and crunchy cookies. We were excited, playing with ideas, the two Peters and myself. The villagers went home, optimistic about the next day's prospects.

By the third day, only five students arrived, and by the last day, day five, only two appeared. I wasn't going to be phased by this. I was going to make the 20 boxes promised but keep them for myself. If the villagers wanted their boxes, they would construct them themselves. They'd been trained, the last thing I wanted was to dish out boxes that they would go out and sell at the Mpulungu market.

By the end of the training, what they wanted from me was clear. The villagers wanted me to make the boxes and employ them. All they wanted was a job. So we tried to get the last three attendants to understand that it was meant to empower them; each one would have a box of their own and then build upon these boxes.

I had 20 boxes made, hung in my forest and made it clear that

I was eager to help anyone interested in setting up boxes for themselves. I'd buy the honey off them. I think that was the last discussion I had with them. A few days later, a few of them pitched up to ask if I could employ them. They weren't interested in setting up their businesses. It seemed to be a repetition of a lot that I'd seen in the villages.

'Give us a job, Madam. Please, a job.' I'd heard this over and over again. Very few were entrepreneurial; they did not want the responsibility of running their own business. It seemed to me that the people preferred to be managed and, in fact, wanted that.

Taking an evening trip into the Kalambo River, my staff and I saw at least three baby crocodiles. This was unusual, crocodiles were rarely seen. We assumed that a female had laid her eggs within the area, and they had hatched. We could expect a few more little creatures in the lake. Generally, crocodiles preferred the dirty, swampy waters of the rivers, but once the crocodile had reached an age where it needed more food, particularly meat, it then began to move into areas where there were dogs, cats, ducks, and children.

The villagers were vigilant around this area and had no sympathy around crocodiles. Daily we heard of more crocodiles being hunted down and killed. As much as I felt this was morally wrong, I made no attempts to save the crocodiles. Ideally, the crocodiles should be transported to Nsumbu Game Reserve, but who was going to do this. If funds weren't found and expertise unavailable, the crocodiles had no chance.

The market in Mpulungu had improved its variety of produce. I could buy guavas, avocados, lemons, and apples. The villagers started to deliver bananas to my home. To my surprise, I found garlic and ginger in the market. With fresh garlic and ginger, there was so much more I could do and experiment with. It felt more and more like home. Even though I loved the place, I still needed my annual holidays in Europe and abroad.

June 2017

June came, and the winds were heavy, loud and angry, especially at night. There was no fish around, not even for the pot. If I wanted fish, I'd have to go into Mpulungu. My honey boxes were finally ready for hanging. When the wax arrived, we smeared it in the boxes to attract the bees. If we placed them in June, our first harvest could be November.

I spent my time putting my notes together for 'The Beautiful Ones Are Born.' Peter occupied himself with adding more pillars to the deck, an additional room as an office or artillery. We hoped to have the building and concrete work completed by July. This would allow a team from Lusaka to complete the roofing. I was going to take advantage of Angelika's team while she was away on holiday in Europe.

Sometime in June, a mad dog roamed into our yard. Little Sunshine, my half min-pin-poodle, attacked it and got badly bitten. My poor darling, trying to protect me. We assumed the stray dog had rabies, so we had to rush Sunshine to the vet in Mpulungu. The vet was keen to see the stray dog. He recommended we kill it and bring the head in for examination. Unfortunately, no one had a gun, so the staff stoned the dog to death. We had no choice. The dog was biting children in the village and now Sunshine.

There was no medicine. We had to keep watch on Sunshine and if she showed any signs of madness within two weeks, we'd have to kill her. The dog had also bitten a little girl, she was also told by the clinic in Mpulungu that she'd have to wait. There was a shortage of medication, and in any case, they only administered the rabies medication, only if they were sure that the patient had the illness. It was such a painful course to take and expensive too.

I loved Sunshine, but given the scenario, I prepared myself to put her to sleep. I wasn't going to wait until it was too late, any signs of abnormality, we'd rush to the vet. He could put her to sleep decently. However, the little girl's situation was more difficult to stomach. Her father rushed her to Kasama General Hospital, where he was told the same thing. Disillusioned, he returned and waited.

The dog was stoned and the head delivered to the vet, who did nothing about it. I suspect it got thrown into the bin. Sunshine got better with a slightly shifted chin, but you could hardly notice. The little girl sparkled two weeks later, ending the dog's saga with rabies.

Peter and I sometimes watched DSTV in the evenings. There were elections in the United Kingdom. The election that Theresa May had pushed forward had backfired on her, putting her in a much weaker position. It looked as though she'd have to resign. We sat with Peter chatting about how Britain was trying so hard to be great again, and it simply was not happening. Britain was not great anymore.

One early morning, the villagers came with a screaming baby otter. I accused them of killing the mother, so I wasn't keen to buy it. Finally, I agreed because I wanted to return it to the water. We agreed at K50. The poor thing screamed and screeched. We tried time and time again to release it into the water, but it was far too young. It kept holding tight to the wall of the rocks and trying to get out. When we wanted to grab it, it snapped at us quite viciously. After hours of exhaustion, it finally allowed Philemon, one of my fish experts, to take it out of the water. We put it in a pen that Toby had built for the crocodiles he had kept. I looked for a feeding bottle, which wasn't easy to find, but in the meantime, the tired little thing had gone silent.

After an hour's nap, when I returned to the pen, Philemon told me that a family of otters had come into the bay. He returned the baby otter to the mother. I knew he was lying; the creature must have ended up in someone's pot. Nevertheless, I was in no mood to argue and chose to accept the lie.

It was 16 June, the month halfway gone already. We woke up to a green lake. The villagers called it 'green water,' something they witnessed annually, sometimes more often at Isanga Bay and Tukulungu for the first time.

It turned out to be cyanobacteria, which apparently had started in the Mpulungu area two days earlier. For two days, you couldn't swim. It looked like sludge all around the jetty caused by water pollution, I was told. A couple of days later, after heavy winds at night, the sludge was washed away by the lake itself. At Isanga Bay, they often got it more than twice a year. It was so bad the only way they could clear it was to bring in the villagers to remove the sludge physically.

July was here faster than I could count to 30, the year I turned 60. I wanted to be at my spiritual centre in France for my sixtieth birthday, and most of all, I wanted to be with my son. I hoped to take this opportunity to tell him that we'd been medicating him in order to calm him as well as explain that he had been diagnosed as bipolar.

I was in Lusaka before jetting off for England and then France. Michael agreed to be in France at the Bonfin for my 60th birthday. It was going to be his birthday present to me, and he did pitch up on my birthday, in France.

I was away for three weeks while Peter took care of the place. The Swiss students were coming for most of the summer, first a small group then a larger group to follow. A few students remained at the lodge to monitor the experiments. We were busy that winter.

I rushed my break and was back before the end of July to host

Andy Andersen, a prominent, successful businessman from Lusaka. We had incredible nights, listening to Elvis Presley and chatting about old times, drinking excellent wine and cooking the most succulent dishes.

The fish in the ponds started dying. Isaac reported that this often happened when the waters got too cold and when the 'green water' came into the bay. I had some students around who inspected the gills and found that the fish had tuberculosis. They gave me all kinds of instructions to wash down the ponds. I asked Isaac what Mr Toby would do, and he instructed me to get tetracycline immediately, then clean the ponds down with coarse salt. It was a lot of work, and I couldn't get any tetracycline in Mpulungu. I was forced to travel to and from Kasama in one day. Immediately, the fish responded and we soon started washing down the ponds and changing the water.

The student around was unhappy because of the tetracycline used that would feedback into the lake. However, considering the volume of water in the lake the small amount of tetracycline used, I really couldn't imagine any genuine concern. The fish were safe and in the end, I lost about 30 instead of the possibility of losing them all.

My relationship with Peter had crumbled. We were distant but entertained the students, and he loved the company of Andy Andersen, who spent a week with us. They could discuss music all night long and listen to oldies.

A few days later, my dear friend Tash came to visit. I think this was the final straw, I had my friend to gossip with and he, one of the students. After this visit, I asked him to start preparing his things to leave. The situation was getting tense and uncomfortable for everyone around.

As the winds calmed, the clarity of the lake returned, that emerald green clarity I'd fallen for year after year. The nightmare of washing down the ponds with coarse salt continued throughout the month, ensuring that every pond was free of the bacteria that had killed the fish in the ponds. My tropheus duboisi, mabilibili, Ilangi, frontosa, and judliochromis regaini.

As spring showed itself towards the end of August, the warmth immediately improved the condition of the fish and health in the ponds had returned. The fish dashed around, sexing and breeding once again.

The forest had started to change to bright autumn colours, red, yellow and orange. It was still relatively cool, the staunch heat hadn't come in yet, although we could have done with some rain. The freshness of the rainy season at this time would have been desirable.

Peter was still hanging around, how I wished he'd pack his bags and leave. The tension was getting unbearable. I was rushing off to Lusaka to meet my dearest friends, Georgie, Gay, Renuka, Temsy, Shelley, Marie-Paul and others who were flying in from all over the world to celebrate our 60th here in Zambia. All ex-Convent girls, from the years 1969 to 1974, after the celebrations in Lusaka, a small group was coming to the lake with me.

Peter stayed on for all the celebrations at the lake. It was such a special time with friends. Georgie, my longest friend, stayed back and travelled with me to Ndole Bay, Chinsali, and then back to Lusaka, where she took the plane to London.

I met her at seven years old and separated when we were thirteen. Georgie returned to the UK to further her education. Later, when I spent a year in England at a private tutorial college in England, we had reunited and kept in contact into our thirties until one day, a letter wasn't returned.

Thanks to Facebook, many years later, we were in our 50s when we found each other again. The two weeks spent travelling, driving, drinking and smashing bottles of wine in the evenings and reminiscing. We bonded again.

It was so easy like we'd never had all those years apart. These bonds, I've come to believe, are past life acquaintances. I felt so close to Georgie. I missed her dearly when I had to say goodbye once again. Had she not had a little angel, Lily, waiting for her at home, I might have convinced her to spend another month with me.

When my friends departed, Peter had taken the opportunity to jump on the bus with them as they left on a hired, air-conditioned bus. He said no goodbye, not even telling me he was finally packed and left. It came as a relief to find his wardrobe empty, all his clothes gone. The place once more returned to my own peaceful, Shangri-La.

It was 10 October when I got back, after dropping Georgie. My car was loaded from Lusaka with a new generator and shopping I had done in Kasama. I rushed to get back home. A strange, foreign voice had called me, asking for a room for the night, something on the beach. I recognised the voice to be Dutch. It turned out he was Belgian, Flemish. He was waiting for me, at the Waterfront. He biked from Kenya into Tanzania,

Zambia, Zimbabwe and hoped to end in Cape Town, where he'd leave his BMW bike and fly back to Kenya, then his final destination Belgium. I interpreted this to be a new chapter in my life. I would host new kind of guests. Guests that were interesting and adventurous. I was getting known. The place was simply gorgeous, added was its remoteness, its absence of hordes of tourism made it the ideal spot for the adventurous tourist, wanting peace and quiet.

We had three days of fun, evenings filled with chilled white wine on the beach and fabulous meals. I welcomed this visitor. He advised me, recommended the things he felt I needed to do to make the place right. His advice was to go high end. He felt I was wasting my time with the low-end market with the food I served and the place's ambience. His gut was for me to take it to a notch higher.

'We should change the expression of living like a king in Paris, to living like a queen on Lake Tanganyika,' was the note he left in my guest book. He reminded me of what life could be. It could be light, joyful, rejoicing in the sheer beauty of life. Life and relationships had to be lighthearted and easy. I felt the strain I had endured with Peter. The hardship of the Davy case. In both situations, I was trying too hard to make things work. All this hardship in my life had to come to an end. I decided to make a conscious effort to replace my tough life with ease, I hoped.

Michael spent a month in Kasama working for Kasama Sugar Company, designing some engineering manuals. He had asked the psychiatrist if he could have a month without medication to see if he really needed them. The psychiatrist felt it was a good idea, insisting to me that he had to make up his own mind. He couldn't be forced to take any medication.

It would have to come from him, that time. The previous secret medication had been done without consent, but his decision to live on medication would have to be his. I was glad for him to be somewhere quiet and peaceful. He was with a Baha'i family I could trust, and he was working once again, something he needed.

After this month break, Michael was clear that he needed medication. He was quickly feeling lonely and depressed. We returned to Lusaka and visited the psychiatrist who put him on Lithium, a mood stabiliser drug. I guessed, no ups and downs, but levelling him out so that he could get on with life. He was given three different doses, and it was for him to decide what dose was best for him— a low dose, middle dose or high dose. Within a few weeks, he was comfortable with the middle dose.

He was fragile, I could tell, but he was getting on with life in a calmer fashion, not the erratic way I had found him a year earlier.

I was heading off to London for the World Tourism Market (WTM), so I'd be away for two weeks. When I got back, Michael was in such a good place. I was sure he'd be alright and get used to the medication and come to terms with the fact that he'd have to live on medication for the rest of his life. Something that wasn't easy for him to accept.

Michael had been having problems with his father. All he ever wanted was to help his father in the business. He had been brought up believing he would run the family business for his dad one day. Unfortunately, his mind wasn't stable, so venturing into new things disoriented him. He wanted stability, and working with his dad was part of that.

Dad was more interested in his latest new catch, young girls, black girls; the younger the better it appeared. He didn't get on with his father's new girlfriend. They often fought. I was exhausted with the subject, and I advised him to leave his father alone and start his own life.

By the time I got back from the WTM, Michael had bought his

ticket to London to start a new life. I was so happy for him. He had looked into various engineering possibilities, in addition with the possibility of moving to Switzerland.

'It's your freedom, darling. I know you'll be happy,' I said to him.

'I'm never coming back here again, I'm gone.'

'Don't worry sweetie, once you have children, you'll really appreciate this place again.'

'With a wife and children, maybe.'

We laughed and chatted to the airport. I dropped Michael off with one last kiss and a hug. Then, he was off to London for a new beginning.

I got back to the lake on 9 December, the rains had begun, and the place was lush green. Tiger Face, my cat, had settled in with the dogs. The dogs had suddenly become vicious against any stranger entering the yard, anger I hadn't seen before. The final straw was when they bit a young boy. I had to rush him to the clinic for antibiotics. I took drastic measures to keep the villagers out of the yard and insisted they use the path we had made for them behind the lodge. It suited me to push them away from my privacy and private beach.

On 16 December, I had a guest for three days. Heinz, one of the older German researchers, the 'lone rider', I called him. He arrived every year, sometimes twice travelling with a group of Zambians he hired. He sailed in a wooden dhow with his crew. Each year, he slept in all the bays along the lake, wherever he could get permission. He explored different bays and studied the cichlids in each bay.

He had a collection of over 50 aquariums at his home in Basel. He represented the cichlids' hobbyists. He braved depraved conditions yearly, camped on beaches, or slept on the dhow. His arrival at the lodge was a treat. I took a cold bottle of decent South African Sauvignon Blanc out of my crystal glasses. I prepared some exquisite fish dishes. When the students came as groups, I tried to keep things basic, but we dined in style in small groups or alone. That was my special treat to them and to myself.

I spent most of my time trying to fill up the ponds with different varieties of cichlids from around our bay. I noticed the researchers' appreciation when they arrived to find fish that were practically extinct in the lake or hard to come by that I now bred in the ponds. I added cat fish that we caught within my bay, hiding under rocks. I added altolanprologus, black in colour, but distinguished as a show piece, and the Solomon fish, a very snake-like looking fish.

The tropheus duboisi were breeding well. They were spotted as fingerlings, their distinction. Then turned striped yellow and blue. At this point, they were both striped and spotted, identified as juveniles. Finally, showing off their maturity when they eventually define their colour as striped blue and yellow.

This distinguished variety, the tropheus dubois, will never mix. Placed with any other species, even very close to it, they do not mix. They mixed and sexed amongst themselves. I called them the racists, the puritans.

The tropheus ilanji, I was told was practically extinct in the lake, so I guarded them well and ensured that we kept them separate. The duboisi you could place with any other breed, they simply would not mix with other fish. The fish we kept would often become mixed breeds that collectors were not interested in.

These mixed breeds became food for Percy, my magnificent,

yellow predator, my Golden Nile perch. With certain fish, and Percy was one, they'd change their sex according to the scarcity of the opposite sex. Percy changed his or her sex whenever he felt like it, so it was difficult to determine whether to call him, he or she. Percy, and finally knighted, Sir Percy, he became, because he was aggressive enough. His aggressive behaviour was masculine, so male he became to us all.

Toby had caught Percy as a baby, 40m underwater. He tried to get him a mate, but each mate was killed or eaten, so finally, they decided to leave him alone. He must have been around 25 years old when I took over the place. No one knew enough about the Golden Nile perch. All we knew was that Percy had albinism. He was the albino Nile perch. He was bright yellow in colour instead of the silvery, grey colour of the average Nile perch. His actual size we'll never really know because fish adapt their size according to the volume of water they're placed in. Given his tank, in comparison to the volume of water in the lake, he'd never grow to the size he might have grown to in his natural habitat. On the other hand, given his bright yellow colour and with no camouflage techniques, he probably would be dead by now.

We were close to Christmas. I noticed the first sand crater against the rocks. Heinz explained that they were the aulonocranus dewinti, where the male of this species constructs a small sandcastle against a small rock. Similarly, the callochromis macrops formed sandcastles in underwater beaches but relatively shallow water, where it was warm. They then led the females to these bowels to spawn.

Close to Christmas, Fred Phiri and a film crew arrived to do a tourism production documentary featuring the lake. The idea was to visit all the lodges and places of interest on the Zambian side. Like so many Zambian productions, everything is dependent on improvisation and the time given. Lack of funds is always a challenge, so I offered to assist with my recently acquired wooden dhow.

The dhow I had designed, with a dining area, tented cover, cushions and a mattress. We got the bottle of sparkling wine out, cold beers, Sauvignon Blanc, some snacks and we were off to Ndole for the night. We hoped to cover all the bays, Kasaba, Nsumbu Game Reserve, Nkamba Bay, Ndole and more.

The trip ended up being one of those where everything went wrong. First, we turned into a bay, no one could recognise. We discovered that we were in the Democratic Republic of Congo. Thomas, the coxswain, spoke Swahili and asked where we were. Luckily, the villagers were friendly and guided us out of the bay, where the authorities would not spot us. What we had done risked us being locked up and taken as spies. We followed the advice given and soon found ourselves back in Zambian waters.

Everything seemed fine. We spent a night in Ndole Bay. I managed to negotiate some perks for the crew, given that it was a documentary they were shooting that we could all benefit from. The next day, we planned a fast exit hoping to follow the route along the coast to Kapembwa and Mpulungu. We said our goodbyes. The weather looked good when we left. But within fifteen minutes of departing Ndole Bay, we were hit with a storm that no one could have predicted.

The winds were so strong the roof and all its wooden structures came flying off. The nails and split timber were exposed, the crew screamed and hid under tables, while Thomas skillfully cut and ripped the tent. As soon as I saw what he was doing, I followed suit and assisted in tearing the tent. I folded it to avoid gathering any wind, which had the potential to tip us over.

The wood where the engine was attached had given us trouble at Ndole Bay. Craig, the owner of Ndole Bay used his carpenters to reinforce the wood where the engine was held.

We discovered that the wood used was not Mukwa, the dark, hardwood generally used for boats. A lot of the wood used to make my boat was of inferior material. I was furious with the boat maker and the group that had convinced me to buy the boat. It seemed that no one could be trusted. If interrogated, they'd all say, 'But we thought you knew, we didn't know that you don't know.'

Stuck in the storm, I watched Thomas tremble because, for once, he had to be honest that the boat wasn't made from Mukwa, and we were all in danger. If the storm got any stronger, the boat would crack and we would drown. We were close to Kapembwa, the home of the goddess of the lake. The Spirit was known to anger very quickly, particularly with men, if the moral laws of the land were broken.

Somehow, I felt that in this incident, Kapembwa was on my side. She wanted the truth revealed that I had been cheated. My crew all knew that Kapembwa angered with men. Her sympathy lay with ladies. Some time ago, the last recorded date was about 100 years ago, virgins were pushed over the cliff to appease the Spirit.

All I wanted at this point was to be on land. We were all soaked and started to shiver as it was getting cold. Fortunately, the engine kept going, and we slowly drifted into Kasaba Bay.

The place was lined with soldiers. However, the soldiers were kind to us and helped us off the boat and assisted us in removing the frame that held the tented cover. The only danger was the split timber, exposed nails and torn tent that had the potential to gather wind and tip us over. The boat stood firm. As the storm subsided, the lake suddenly became still. We had another three hours on the water.

We had a chance to either head back to Ndole and spend the night there or head home. Everyone wanted to get home. We travelled in silence. At last, we could see the lodge. At this point, some of the crew started crying.

Thomas's assistant screamed with excitement as tears ran down his cheeks. 'Never, never again. Never. That was Kapembwa, now I know. It's true, Kapembwa is dangerous, never, never again!'

The boat was damaged. The next day, the documentary crew rushed to Mpulungu and rushed home. The tent was taken to the tailor in Chipwa, Tanzania, who did a good job of mending it. The boat was demoted to sunset cruises and was not allowed for long trips, not even to Mpulungu.

It was established that most of the boat was actually made from another dark wood, similar to mukwa but softer. I had been crooked, and everyone agreed. The boatmen were all reprimanded by their fellow Lungus. Everyone felt guilty for putting us all through death's door. For the first time, I think, I felt a sense of commitment from the community for my well-being and the well-being of all the people I employed.

The rains were here, pouring down consistently, and the jetty was full of cichlids. All my children were coming home for Christmas except Michael. He was away in London. I sent him a message on WhatsApp.

Everyone will be here for Christmas. What I miss most is your presence, how I wish you could be here with us. I love you, my baby.

I love you too, mummy, he replied.

The snakes had started moving around. December, the first rains, was always the time for snakes. I spotted a yellow tiger snake, it was a baby and decided to leave it alone. The next day we found it in one of the chalets. The staff came screaming and squashed its head. 'This is a very dangerous snake.' It was exactly the same one I'd seen on my window sill and I decided to leave it alone. 'Good God,' I thought, you could not tell what was dangerous, poisonous or not.

Some lodges would never kill a snake, venomous or not. They redirected the snake back into the bush. My experience was that they always came back. The policy I adopted for the lodge was if we found a dangerous snake in the rooms, dining area or kitchen, we killed it. If found in the forest, we left it alone and only venomous snakes, we'd kill. The innocent, sand, bush, garden, house, green snakes, we left alone, to mingle with us, if they cared to.

Quite frankly, I don't think I ever got completely used to having snakes as part of my garden but my fear towards them was deeply removed. From the town girl of Lusaka who killed any snake I saw, I started appreciating their presence, watching them sometimes chase a lizard or gecko, which weren't an easy feat for the snake. The lizards were fast, hiding behind crevices and pictures on the wall which dazzled the snake, it was so cute to watch.

We had Christmas with the family; Gloria invited her Turkish friend. It was different from the perfection of two years ago when I had the whole family, including my son-in-law's family. That year the group was smaller— Gloria, Angelika, Tue, Erik, my grandson all came, including Gloria's friend from Turkey.

Christmas passed, the family departed, I knew I had to make that trip to London. I had to be with Michael, my soul and heart could not rest.

JANUARY 2018

My son was no more. He had taken his own life, alone in London.

APRIL 2018

Hope

When Michael passed over to the other side, I couldn't cope. I took a year off, visiting spiritual centres and travelling while trying to make sense of my life. I called a missionary friend, Lynn, to run the place while taking time off to recover, gather strength and get my life back.

'It will be difficult for me,' she replied, 'but I do have my daughter, Hope, a nineteen-year-old, who's just completed school. I think she could do it. She's young but very mature and pretty capable. I think she'd be delighted to hold the fort. She's very competent.'

That's all I needed to hear, Hope was hired. I had no judgement or discernment. All I wanted was to leave and let someone take care of the place for me while I roamed.

I was with Gloria, who kept close to me and ensured that I was alright and in safe hands. We took the boat over to Mpulungu to pick Hope up.

Hope was sweet, pretty, innocent and kind with a delightful smile. She was young, had sparkling eyes, jet-black curly hair and tanned skin. I wished my son was around; *he would have fallen for this beauty, this cutie, she could twist every heart,* this one. What a pity, what a sweetie, life could be so cruel.' I had myriad thoughts, feelings, and emotions as this gazelle stepped onto the boat.

'You're so pretty.' I couldn't help myself saying. She giggled, her smile shone, and the freckles twitched. They looked like little stars all over her face.

Every student loved Hope, and clients warmed to her. Guests would often ask, 'How old is Hope, may we guess? Let's guess!' Compliment after compliment followed, her youth became a source of inspiration. She brought her friends, her parents' friends, the Mbala farmers, the Serenje farmers, and she filled the place with joy. All the young lads fell in love with her. She had a clear idea of what she was looking for.

She said, 'A Christian, a man-man. A man who can fix and

repair things, sort things out. I have my checklist. They have to tick the boxes.'

It still did not stop the lads from trying, and she turned them all away.

'He's got to fit the profile and tick all boxes. I don't want to end up in Europe, I'm African, and I want to live in Africa. I'm not interested in anyone who wants to take me away, I'm African.'

'Good God,' I said, 'you have all the possibilities and chances of marrying a Swiss, a German, why choose someone who'll keep you here. You're young, travel the world, have fun, explore, grow wings.' I tried to persuade her.

'I love Africa and I'm not leaving.'

My opinions were not welcomed or entertained. Hope had very strong ideas about life and where she was going, and it certainly was not going to be abroad or going to university. Marriage was a sacred union to her, and sex before marriage was out of the question.

We loved each other, like mother and daughter. She enjoyed decorating the table with crystal glasses and fine china. She dressed up for each meal, she had a conservative and vintage style.

It wasn't long before prince charming arrived. The son of a Serenje farmer, the Sheriff family. He was tall, handsome and blue-eyed. He was a fixer and a Zambian farmer. Her life was guaranteed in Zambia. The cherry on the top, the young lad was Christian and he ticked every box.

'You have no idea how happy you make me,' she wrote on her Facebook page. I knew from then on that my delightful days with Hope were coming to an end.

Exactly a year later, she resigned and chose life in Serenje. A special time had come to an end. Hope had held the fort for me while I was away. This time was soon over, far too soon for me. She was sent to me at such a difficult time in my life to bring me hope, as her name suggested, and to hold the fort while I gathered strength.

APRIL 2019

I came back to the lake to decide my next move. I spent two months alone, sitting on my old wicker chairs by the beach. The sand oozed between my feet.

Would I go rustic, with metal jugs on the beach, rattling, heating up in the blazing sun, sweating in peoples' arms, or keep the beach plastic? Redecorate the place, change the theme? I needed to make changes. Improvements were needed. An injection of colour, decor design, my enthusiasm was failing me, yet it was clear, the place needed change.

I made a trip to Mpulungu. All I could notice was the forlorn sight of the dingy market, a hideous monument for Mpulungu. All unsightly, imposing, an eyesore, that's all I could focus on.

What I needed now was a semblance of order and beauty, not the surrounding chaos I saw—perhaps, reflecting my inner chaos of emotions and confusion. I wasn't ready to face my inner confusion, so projecting it onto everything around me.

The Mpulungu heat was like a sauna. At home, I coped with it by sleeping through the heat. Then as the day cooled off, I'd walk my dog Matata, his mate Hakuna had been put to sleep by Hope after developing an incurable knee infection. I gave Sunshine to Hope. My life was that of a vagabond, keeping still and staying in one place felt wrong or too difficult for me to bear. It felt uncomfortable and painful. I needed to keep moving.

With Matata, I began my forays into the forest searching for the last mushrooms of the season. I sifted through rotten fallen leaves. *Oh, they do taste so much better once you pick them yourself*, I thought. They looked closer to the European chanterelles, hard and easy to dry. The locals usually dried and stored them for when they were out of season.

The first mushrooms appeared in November after the first heavy rain. There were different varieties throughout the season. November was *tente*, the small round slimy mushrooms. What followed was the large umbrella-shaped mushrooms. End of December and into January and February, three different varieties were predominant, your little red and yellow mushrooms, *sweta*, they called them here, and the small brown mushrooms, *chibesa*, my favourite. February to the end of the rains were the different chanterelle varieties.

The north was a paradise for mushroom lovers. We had six months of mushroom picking and trying different ways to cook, pickle, and appreciate the mushrooms. This year, my *joie de vivre* escaped me. I gathered the mushrooms and handed them over to the staff. I lost the excitement for things. I needed someone to hold the fort once again.

I soon found some temporary help. Ryan came for three months, Peter, my ex, lived on the lake close to me. He looked after the place over the summer so I could stay longer in Europe. I hoped to return in October with renewed inspiration and enthusiasm because I knew I loved the place. It had deeply grown into my soul; neither could I give it up nor sell it.

Mpulungu, originally Pu'lungu, meant 'give me beads,' perhaps during the slave trade when beads were used as a means of trade. The port is where a lot of trade took place. Tukulungu, the spot I was on, meant, 'I take all the beads.' Alternatively, 'tuku,' meaning the place of the Lungu people who resided there. According to the headman, Happy, the white man struggled to say, Pu'lungu, which one day became, Mpulungu. I enjoyed Happy's explanation when he came over to visit. He hoped I was back to stay. I told him I lived on the spot called

Tukulungu, I own it, 'I, take all the beads, I want it all, all for myself. I'm here to stay, just give me time.' I begged.

OCTOBER 2019 - APRIL 2020

Surviving

I was back at the lake in October 2019. Peter had held the fort for me while I spent more time in France, praying, fasting, meditating, and working at a spiritual centre, Le Bonfin, in Côte d'Azur. I ended up in the domain of food. I was assigned the responsibility for *la pluche*, the place where all the cleaning and preparation for the kitchen goes on. I was weighing the food, washing it, cutting and chopping, directing and giving instructions in French. Summer in Europe came to an abrupt end, sooner than I wanted. I comfortably could have spent another year in that role. I was happy and felt stronger to face the world again.

I had been communicating with Julie, the mother of my son's best friend, Ranen. We had met at the celebration of Michael's life and somehow developed a warm relationship together. She had agreed to give the lake a shot, spend some time at the lake and see if she could run it for me.

Julie

Julie warmed to the place, the sheer beauty of it. She was spellbound, but her fear was the isolation and her own confidence to manage the place. Julie was loving, caring, my age, in her sixties and very attractive. She kept her body trim and ensured she didn't over eat, to a point where I wondered if she had an eating disorder. Her meals were sometimes a spoon of peanut butter and half a boiled egg. *Well, this one will certainly not eat me out of house and home,* I secretly thought.

She was gentle, fragile, full of love and compassion. The staff were loved, and she knew everyone's name and got to know everyone's personal history. Julie loved the children in the village, adored the teachers, the nurses, and the headman, and was involved in the school projects. Every Sunday, she attended the little village church and came back mesmerised by the people's voices. I named her Mother Theresa.

She found her passion in the garden, the church and the staff. Unfortunately, the place was too quiet, the storms were aggressive, the rains heavy and people in general did not move around. I had grown accustomed to this; January and February were always tricky, daily rain kept people from travelling. Yet, it was the time I most enjoyed.

By March 2020, isolation and loneliness had taken their toll on Julie. She was offered another job at the Lower Zambezi as a private teacher for two children, and she decided to take the offer up. Even though she was unsure if she was making the right decision, she needed company. We were also just at the beginning of the coronavirus pandemic, and its uncertainty added to her fear. She left in March 2020.

Within a month, I received mail from both Basel and Graz universities stating that they were not sure of their movements that year. Next was National Geographic, who had planned a second documentary of the lake. Their first one, 'Little Fish in Deep Water,' had been such a success. They planned to upgrade and spend time at Kalambo Falls Lodge, shooting.

I loved the first video and couldn't imagine how they could improve anything that was so magnificently captured. I was excited and looked forward to their arrival, but the trip was also postponed. A Mercedes Benz 4x4 tour was also postponed or cancelled. The list of cancellations and postponements went on. Perhaps Julie made the right decision. The loneliness would have possibly destroyed her. The place was dead.

In an interim period, Julie was quickly replaced by a Zambian lady, Mwansa. She was young, pretty and perfectly capable of running the place and keeping it tidy. It was all I needed. The country and the whole world went into lockdown. All we could do was drift, and sailing we did, as Mwansa managed the place.

Covid-19 had taken over every conversation. I put away any ideas of making money; covering the bills was all that mattered. The place needed a huge injection of capital for renovations but was it worth the expense?

I had planned my trip to France in April, but even that was halted. I was grounded, which gave me plenty of time to reflect and my God, how lucky I was to be grounded in paradise. The communication connectivity at the lake had improved. So it felt more like "paradise connected" no longer isolated and cut off in paradise.

BEGINNING APRIL 2020 - JANUARY 2021

The Coronavirus

I met Mwansa for the first time in April. I oriented her to the place. It felt like musical chairs, travelling up and down, Lusaka, Chinsali and the lake. The driving had become exhausting. Travelling abroad was almost impossible. President Edgar Lungu announced a partial lockdown. Fear spread like wildfire; when I travelled, I turned the radio on and off. Over this period, I listened to updates while I travelled.

Coronavirus prevention messages started appearing on all billboards. It was headline news on radio, television, Facebook, and other social media. Everything centred around this infectious disease.

'What's going to happen to us, Madam? How do we know we have corona?' The staff panicked, what did I know.

'It's like a flu or cold, *chifuba*. It's nothing to worry about; just treat it like *chifuba*,' I said.

The place had poor medical facilities. The villagers would be the last to get attended to anyway, so best for me and the villagers, was to go back to the way I had been brought up, a concoction of hot lemon and honey, I added garlic and ginger to my recommendations.

The more I read about it and delved into anything I could find, it was clear that most people developed a mild to moderate respiratory illness and recovered without requiring special treatment. So I underplayed the pandemic, intuitively knowing it was the best way to go. Panic and fear would only exasperate the situation, and there was no point.

These villagers were strong and healthy, and their diet contained lots of fish and wild vegetables. They couldn't afford junk food. They walked everywhere and were physically fit. Their young ages also worked in their favour. I hoped and prayed.

To me, Coronavirus became the metaphor for what was going on in the world at large. Our world had become diseased. Our thoughts, feelings, and emotions had been taken over. They were hijacked by greed, jealousy, selfishness and hate. The desire for money and power had ceased the world.

The coronavirus was simply a manifestation on the physical plane of what had already happened on the mental and emotional levels. It had descended to the physical as a disease that attacked our lungs and ability to breathe and hence our ability to love and feel.

Ironically, the words 'herd immunity' were used to define the direction World Health Organisation wanted for us. The use of the term upset my bowels.

Why use the word herd? Were we animals? Cows? For God's sake, what had become of this world? A world where we perceived each other like animals and no one seemed to question the use of the word herd, I thought. Call it a community, immunity of the community or community-immunity it would be more compassionate, not a bunch of animals.

My cells were filled with a worrying chill as I analysed and assessed my own life and the world I was living in. I was afraid to say the wrong thing in public. I watched accepted conversation styles and was constantly afraid of being politically incorrect. This had become a pattern for me.

Were our perceptions being controlled? I had to question myself. Who was controlling our perceptions? The media, social media? If our perceptions were now being controlled, then who was behind it? Who was moulding us? Who or what was behind it? It's clear that our behaviour is a result of our perceptions. It's so important to safeguard our perceptions.

The danger lies in that, as a society, we are guided by our perceptions. If those perceptions are now controlled by social media, controlled by an accepted convention or norm, then, as a society, we had to question how free we were.

Society, as we know it today, is totally guided by social media. That, for me, had become 'a truth,' a realisation that we were controlled and guided in a certain direction. A certain way of thinking and behaving. Was this what I wanted? Was it a direction I wanted to continue pursuing? I started questioning myself, my life, our life, in so many different ways I had never thought about before.

We were grounded. All we had was social media to listen to and connect us. All I knew for sure now was that I wanted change. I'm sure this is the way we were all thinking as collective beings. We all wanted CHANGE! Something had to happen. Something had to give in. We all wanted change and coronavirus, brought the occasion, to access what life we wanted for ourselves.

Social media was rife. We all had access to it. We shared, we shouted, we screamed, we cried, we voiced our opinions via social media, Facebook, Twitter, WhatsApp, and Instagram are all channels where we could share our perceptions, thoughts, fears, hopes and dreams.

We were all under lockdown, house arrest, 'with no crime,' the whole world, it seemed, the lockdown continued, extended. 'No crime?' My mind went from one thing to another.

On second thought, our crime was to worship the god of money, power, the god of nonsense, trivia, image, superficiality, the god of trouble and destruction. Was there not another god, a god of love, beauty, joy, compassion, health, happiness and bliss?

We all longed to meet again. We chatted on Zoom, WhatsApp chats and video calls, but it wasn't the same. We longed to be able to touch each other, hug and kiss, be in the same room, drink a bottle of wine together. We made plans of what we'd do when the pandemic was over, 'India, Sri Lanka once again, no Zambia, where we all met,' we lived for promises, wishes and dreams, for better times, to meet again, for NORMALITY, once again.

As I settled down at the lake again in January 2021, we heard of a new mutation. South Africa went into lockdown, Zimbabwe too. All we could do was wait for what would come next. From desperately wanting normality, the new word I constantly heard was CHANGE. We need change, and everybody wants change. Whatever that change meant, change became the new word. Change!

November 2020

BUYANTANSHI, I lost my son on 1 January 2018, New Year's Day. Life changed. I wrote a booklet called 'Journey of the Soul.' All I could do was think of him, dream of him and connect to him. I lived in and out of this world. Finally, lying on my back, spread-eagled, my eyes to the sky, I knew I was back. I was 63 years old, no excuse to give up. There was plenty that life offered. I had a beautiful home, I had created beauty all around me, and I was living the eternal spring.

I had once read that melancholy, was in fact, "the ultimate emotional indulgence." I imagined it was the preserve for the wealthy and privileged. I had no right to stay there. Parallel to my existence of luxury was a large extended family, living in the greatest of simplicity and sheer poverty. They laughed, smiled and danced. Their lives unfolded in front of me as they came in and out, the smell of sweat lingering on long after they left and as they walked away in the sun.

They became my large extended family. They brought me mangoes, bananas, fresh and dried fish, mushrooms, anything in season, then baskets and clay pots. We bargained and negotiated one of us won. 'You're our mother, Madam,' they would say.

Guests came in and out. They hung around on the beach in bikinis wore climbing shoes for the trek to Kalambo Falls. They read, gossiped, partied and indulged in my cuisine. Sometimes, we got on each other's nerves. Other times people fell in love and proposed. The privileged life of luxury and indulgence.

My eyes fought a furious battle as I hauled the duvet off me. The sun had come over the hill, its reflection on the water. A rainbow which I considered my symbol of life, appeared. It made a bow over the inland lake. The wind hit my face, and I felt alive again. I plunged into the lake. My voice was no longer a whisper but loud and clear, each word well pronounced. My Bemba improved too.

My home, my roots were now in Chinsali. My son's memory would live forever, "A Garden of Peace," I started creating for him from about October 2019, when I had returned from France. I moved from Lusaka, Chinsali and the lake but used my time in Chinsali to grow more roots there.

In Chinsali, I could garden, I could turn the soil, I found comfort in this, I used this time to transform my pain. It soon started feeling like home. It's where my mother, my grandmother came from. It was my roots, after all.

15 November 2020

My life was divided between Chinsali and the lake. I arrived in Chinsali and drove through my 'boulevard.' Dried stumps of trees lined the avenue, the entrance to my home. I had used burnt down stumps, trees cut, massacred, and rescued to give them a permanent home. My driveway I decorated with stumps. I called the alley leading to my house "the cry of the forest." A reminder of the deforestation that was threatening the nation. The loss of all-out indigenous, tropical forests to tree poachers, who exported the aged dark woods to China. Others were destroyed by villages desperate for food and grain, still using old traditional methods of farming, the famous chitemene system, where the burning of trees was still used as fertilisers. As a result, every year, forests disappeared either for export to China or turned into charcoal or stumped and burnt as fertiliser.

The rains had just begun. The air smelt of dust and smoke from the burnt forests.

'You've brought us luck, Madam. You've come with the rain. It's your presence, Madam, you're bringing us life and blessings.

'The future, Madam, you've brought us the future! *Buyantanshi*.'

Any form of development was termed, *buyantashi*. This word always brought smiles, laughter and hope. Everywhere I travelled in the north, the word echoed, *buyantashi*, a future of development, they all dreamt.

My staff gave me a warm welcome. I could hear a dull thunder, another storm brewing in the distance. My little red tractor came roaring and stopped abruptly so that the driver could greet me with respect, taking his hat off as he greeted me.

Everyone was smiling, glad to see me back. The staff from the house came hopping like rabbits to carry the luggage and all the fresh food I had bought from Shoprite Kasama on my way to Chinsali. This was the only supermarket in the north.

I remembered the first time I'd visited the north, now nearly ten years ago. I spotted a supermarket, Shoprite. It was like finding gold, and I was jumping and singing, 'Shoprite!' For the first time in my life, I understood what it must mean to the villages when a new hypermarket arrives in town. Suddenly, you could get fresh bread and butter, jams, yoghurt, granola, a further treat, cheese, olives, and olive oil. It was wonderful. Shoprite brought Christmas to all of us in the rural areas, yes, I suppose, this must feel like *buyantashi*, the future, and it did feel good.

The staff had now stopped hopping and were jumping around. The thunder had followed me. One of the ladies, *Bana* Land, the mother of Land, was feeding the chickens when she spotted me.

A casual or part-time gardener, weeding the newly planned lawn, baby strapped to her back. Young girls, young boys all opted for part-time jobs, digging, planting, weeding and opening of roads. There was an endless cry for jobs.

I was now up to twenty permanent workers in Chinsali and another twenty at the lake, but in reality, I always had about ten additional staff at the lake to help with the buildings going on, a new deck, three new chalets and a whole new camping site, planned for an annual festival.

In Chinsali, it took an additional forty casuals, part-time labourers to assist with the organic vegetables I was experimenting on. We were opening new roads, adding chalets, a camping site, picnic spots still to be built. I needed the energy, the stamina, the health and the money it would entail.

I prayed I was part of this *buyantashi.* The expectation, the neediness in the workers' eyes, the hope, the love, the confidence they had in me kept me going, kept me alive, gave me renewed energy, vitality, enthusiasm I'd never felt before. I couldn't let them down.

I was exhausted, and the sun hit my right hand on the journey to Chinsali. The road was full of potholes and indisciplined truck drivers along the Mpika-Nakonde route. That year the roads had not been repaired. In spite of all the toll gates that were built nationwide, the roads remained a dismal tale of failure.

I argued with the gentleman at the toll gate, 'What are we paying toll fees for? The potholes could comfortably house a pig, a goat, a family of ducks and chickens. Why don't you turn those holes into homes for the animals if you can't repair the roads?'

'Ah, madam, you are funny. The money you are paying us will go to repair the roads next year. We are collecting the money to repair the road.'

There was no point in getting angry or arguing. You'd be delaying your own trip home. Sometimes you'd meet up with someone who took offence, and you could get locked up, fined or delayed for hours.

PAYING AT TOLL GATES IS LAW, the board reminded us all.

When I arrived, it was raining heavily. I ducked indoors, and my cats scrambled with joy as they avoided the staff bringing baggage and food in the house. I frantically started dusting the furniture and window panes. The staff taking care of the house worried that they hadn't done a good job. I rearranged things in the orderly fashion I was accustomed to.

Sometimes we were awkward with each other. I wanted everything in a certain place. They couldn't understand why that was the case. Their world was so different from mine. I hated myself for being so particular. Why didn't I simply compliment instead of spending the first few hours moving and correcting things? I wasn't comfortable and couldn't relax until the home reflected what I wanted. Only when everything was in order could I sit down, relax and open a chilled bottle of white wine or a beer.

'What have you prepared, Ben?' I asked. Ben was the new staff member and I was training him to become a chef. He was brilliant and a fast learner. He had enthusiasm and passion for the kitchen. He filled me with hope. At only 20 years old, he desired to become a chef one day. He spoke a few words of English and could neither read nor write. What he had going for himself was his sense of cleanliness. I trained other young people with the passion and desire in the fields I handled with ease— cooking, cleaning and gardening.

I reflected on their world and mine. My home, the farm, their world, the village, living side by side. Soon to be divided by a fence. For now, nothing but boundaries set, survey diagrams in place, but in reality, nothing really divided us but our different lifestyles.

Our lives couldn't be more different. My life was neat, tidy, organised, structured and beautiful. Beauty had become my living motto. I wanted beauty all around me, flowers in bloom, trees manicured, chopped or trimmed. I wanted colours for all seasons, indigenous bulbs, aloes mixed with imported blossoms, mingled together to give colour all year round.

Life in the village was dirty, the few belongings littered everywhere. I had so much, but everything had its place. They had so little, yet even with the few things they owned, nothing had a place. Everything seemed to be dispersed everywhere, one big mess.

Their fame to cleanliness, a yard swept clean, no lawn, no grass, only sand and dirt to ensure that no snakes felt safe to linger nearby. Their small handmade doors closed at night, their only sense of privacy, yet, within those closed doors slept maybe four people, six, ten, all in a tiny hut. There was no privacy, not even during lovemaking.

My life was all about privacy, being alone. My lounge, dining room, balcony, three bedrooms, and storeroom was all for myself—the estate, the farm, all mine and for my children to inherit one day. Guests, friends and clients came at my discretion. My life was a private one. I loved my quiet moments, time to myself. This the villages could not understand. From time to time, they commuted to come and give me company, sit down, try to make some kind of conversation.

The watchmen, imposing at night, checking to see if they could engage in some chat until finally, I had to explain, 'People like me, we like to be quiet, we like to be alone, to think, we don't like too much company, we don't like to talk too much, we like to be free to think.' This was usually received with, 'Ok, Madam, we shall see you tomorrow,' and sure enough, sometime in the future, they would try again, I guess hoping that I'd at some point get tired of thinking and might want to engage in some conversation.

Sometimes I'd offer them a drink and attempt to practice my now improving Bemba, but I still wished they'd leave me alone. I wondered if I'd ever get tired of gazing over the valley, sipping a glass of cold white wine and simply thinking, contemplating and enjoying the peace, quiet and serenity.

Lusaka buzzed with construction. Everyone was building shopping malls, restaurants, cafes, and bistros. In the ten years I had been away, a lot had changed and I could hardly recognise the place. I kept getting disoriented. New roads had come up, diversions everywhere, one-way traffic and I couldn't stand the noise. The nights were filled with roaring generators or loud music from some nightclub. It reminded me why I loved the bush so much.

The next day my house was full. The director from ZESCO, the electricity company, had come over to visit. He came with the "prime minister to the chief," he called himself Charles Kayula. Sometimes, the Chief came as well, but he had recently fathered a baby girl in his 60s and was doting on her in Lusaka, so we rarely saw him these days.

I loved those days; it felt like a party. With everyone gathered at my home, Charles Kayula played his guitar and sang his favourite folk song I had now heard, perhaps a hundred times.

Tente, the white wild mushroom that has its time.
It bursts into life, lives and then withers and dies.
Such is life! We come to life, we live and we wither and we die.

We all sang, me, in my broken Bemba, but I could join in the song. Charles strummed and sang, joyously drinking his beer, me sipping on my wine and the director, mixing rum and Fruticana, a new brand of fresh fruit juices. I had grown to love my new home in Chinsali. I felt grounded, home, rooted and strong.

The shadows in the night, all alone in my house, never frightened me. I was free to live here, to create my own reality, my own dream. I could be as creative as I wanted. I could paint the pictures in my dreams, weave a new life, the tapestry, the painting of my *buyantashi*.

NOVEMBER 2020

It was late November, once again drawn back to the lake. My Tamba Tamba had disappeared, floated away in a Mpulungu storm. I know they lied to me. We got the police involved, the headman, offered a reward for its return, but all the vain. Finally, I had to make a tough decision and get rid of the management and manage the place by myself for some time. I would then decide whether to sell the business or not. Trying to keep two places operational was definitely not going to work unless I could bring in some decent management. I thought if I chose to keep the place, it would be best to bring in a couple; perhaps the place was too lonely for one person. Unless you owned it, of course.

Gloria flew down from Norway to be with me for two months. I made it clear that if my children, Gloria and Angelika, didn't take an interest in the place, it was best to get rid of it. Sailing back to the spot, Tukulungu, my heart began to melt once again. This time, I tried hard to stay rational. I was going to put it on the market if I couldn't get the place to work.

Over the festive season, Gloria and I scrubbed, painted and decorated the place that by the time 2021 showed itself, I couldn't imagine ever having wanted to sell the place.

The deck that had been staring at me for ages was finally complete. Slowly each piece of furniture I had accumulated over the years found its unique place. The place lost its overcrowded look and a sense of style, Afro-chic returned. What had happened to me was that I'd got so busy that I had stopped looking at the detail. My focus was on getting the place finished, so everything around me was functional rather than stylish. Gloria brought back the sense of flair, attention to detail, chicness and style. The place looked gorgeous. I then focused on the kitchen, worked on the presentation, and added new recipes to the menu.

2021 was now on the horizon, the year I would turn 64. In March, I would have been here for exactly seven years. Seven years reflecting on the lake. I remembered the first time I came here; I was clear at the time that I didn't want to be a prisoner of the place. I was happy to have a holiday home here to enjoy the place but certain that I wanted a manager to run the place.

I wanted the freedom to travel and enjoy other places and destinations. The world was beautiful, and I didn't want to be held captive.

I realised how I didn't enjoy leaving the place. I organised it that Thomas did all the shopping. I rarely went into town or took off for an overnight in Kasama. I organised a little shop in Mpulungu, we called the Pink Shop, to bring me gas and other essentials, like brown flour and dainty soaps for the rooms. Anything I couldn't get in Mpulungu could be sourced for me in Kasama. I was determined to run the place with local produce, which I turned into miraculous food.

More towers had been placed around Mpulungu and Mbala areas so the network got better. Airtel had also introduced a package called 'so che,' with this, I could download movies, documentaries, YouTube and Netflix. There was no need to keep going into town to access good internet.

I missed my annual trips to Europe and perhaps a stint in Asia or South America. All this I wished for but I didn't crave it as much anymore and felt happier growing roots. Perhaps this is what covid had done to me because I had been grounded for a year, unable to leave the country. I was beginning to sink into a home, knowing where my roots belonged. I was convinced that this was where my purpose lay, the last chapter of my life. I was tired of moving and running from here to there.

When the family left on 2 January 2021, I stayed behind. I was glad to be alone, to meditate and plan the year ahead. I wanted to create a large camping area. With covid and lockdown extended, we were getting more and more enquiries from local tourists. We dropped the price of the packages I offered, created all kinds of specials, hoping to keep the place alive. The camping site was essential, and most local tourists were on a tight budget, so plans went ahead to create something creative and affordable that I hoped would bring in more people, chatter and fun.

I had ideas, plans conjuring in my mind. I was home, to my paradise, my Shangri La. I was busy, bubbling through life, full of renewed life and enthusiasm. I planned to get the lake working and put Chinsali on hold. The construction in Chinsali would continue, but I had to delay the opening.

What I needed was to go slowly, to take my steps slower, day by day, there was no hurry. I was soon 64, and my pace was already slowing down, taking every day step by step, discovering what had brought me here and where I could make a significant difference.

JANUARY 2021

Michael, born Josef Niklaus Huwiler

It had been three years since Michael was on the other side. I learned to live without his physical presence, knowing that we were united for all eternity and that I'd be with him again. We would experience each other's lives once again and perhaps travel to different dimensions together. I loved him deeply. He had become the love of my life.

I spent January 2021 at the lake, decorating and preparing the place for the new manager and his wife, who were to take over by mid-March when I would return to Chinsali. I would be returning to Chinsali to prepare for the official opening of my garden of peace, which I planned to do sometime later in the year.

I was going through my bookshelf, and was drawn to a book by William Styron, '*Darkness Visible: A Memoir of Madness*'[1]. I

1 Stryron, W. (1990). Darkness Visible: A Memoir on Madness. New York: Random House.

sat to browse through the book and then I couldn't stop. It was as though Michael had used this book to communicate to me. He wanted me to understand further just how he had felt and for me to understand his act of suicide. I didn't know where the book had come from, and I certainly hadn't bought it. It had no name inside; perhaps a client must have accidentally left it. It didn't matter. The book served as an additional healing instrument for me to understand just what my son had to go through—the depth of his pain and suffering. *Darkness Visible* deepened my awareness of the situation. *Did a client leave it deliberately, afraid to bring up the topic?* I pondered. Whatever the case, it seemed trivial compared to how this book spoke to me. It's a book I highly recommend for anyone dealing with depression.

Michael took his life on 1 January 2018. He had spent the festive season alone. He desperately wanted to get out of Zambia. Michael had many problems with his father, especially with his new girlfriend. The feud had worsened and all he wanted was out. No matter how much I talked to him into staying for Christmas and New Year, he wouldn't barge. He wanted to start a new life and be free from the abuse and humiliation from his father.

In Styron's book, he explains what suffering from a severe

depressive illness feels like. You flounder helplessly in an effort to deal with your state. You are not cheered by the festive season or any form of fun around you. You're going through self-hate, a failure of self-esteem, feelings of worthlessness and as the disorder progresses, this feeling of worthlessness is intensified.

Michael had been a high achiever all his life and received many awards during his school years. However, he had faced and learnt to live with jealousy, backbiting, envy, and I guess from his side, the pleasure and torture, at the same time of receiving or taking all the awards.

I find it odd the jealousy from friends, family and close ones. All those who present a false modesty but stab you in the back. Michael was also naive, as most young people are and never quite understood the difference between compliments and poison, like prayers that can often be curses. The limelight, too often, will often make the ones around you want your place, position, mind and talent.

I remembered the death of John Lennon. He was shot by a lunatic, a madman, who when asked, 'why?' Answered something to the tune of, 'I wanted to be like him, to be loved and admired, like he was, I wanted his place.'

A psychic once told me that jealousy was poison. It was worse than black magic. Black magic you can remove, but jealousy sticks to you like sticky toffee that sometimes is impossible to get rid of. Its energy would only destroy you in the long run.

'Avoid making people jealous of you. It was better to love, but don't tell anybody about it. Make lots of money, do whatever you want, but in silence. Don't tell anyone because people have the habit of spoiling all that is beautiful and perfect,' the psychic said.

Michael suffered from terrible depression and a disorder of mood called bipolar. Unfortunately, they labelled it, a label I detest. I think it's difficult to give a name to all these different states of depression or mood swings. They're all so different and unique to the individual. It's a shame to box them up into labels or label them into boxes. It seems like simplifying a complex, multifaceted medical problem that needs to be seriously further studied and researched.

Perhaps even the idea of delving into different cultures alternative ways of dealing with and addressing mental issues should be welcomed. The route of medication, adding more chemicals to a body and a mind that's already gone crazy due to chemical imbalances, sounds absurd to me today. There must be other methods that need exploration and research.

A further understanding of other cultures and how they deal with mental disorders is essential. Having watched my son deteriorate, I wondered if the medication was, in fact, the catalyst to his suicide.

I planned to explore alternatives to medication as soon as the coronavirus was over. I wanted to take another year off to search the range of alternative and spiritual ways of dealing with mental issues and, specifically, manic depression, what they now call bipolar.

In Styron's book, he explains how he had personally been down this descending spiral and had hit rock bottom. He describes depression as a disorder of mood. A mysterious, painful and elusive illness, known only to itself. He continues saying that it felt like a mediating intellect and suffering beyond description.

The issue with the disease is that if you haven't experienced it, it simply was incomprehensible to the ordinary mind. Styron felt it was utterly indescribable to those who had not experienced it in its extreme mode, and I was one of those.

How could I have possibly understood what my son was going

through? I was always 'Madam positive,' extremely optimistic. Michael's early calls for help, he actually never called for help, literally, but in hindsight, the early symptoms were there. I was a layman to the medical world. I could not have noticed anything too unusual.

I was healthy, always jogged, trekked in the wild and swam. I rarely got sick. During my years with my little children, I don't ever remember giving them pills. Hot lemon juice with honey for flu, a good sleep for headaches, warm prunes for constipation, and as for diarrhoea, they drank herbal teas or hot water. In fact, the runs were a natural way to detox the body. That was about as far as my world of medicine ventured.

He was about 19 years old when the first signs showed. To me, that was normal; it was what most people went through. It was called growing up when for the first time, you're overwhelmed with a sense of responsibility. You contemplate more, think about things and reflect on life. The happy forever period of mummy and daddy taking care of things ends and the beginning of responsibilities rears its ugly head. It's not an easy time, so his sudden pensiveness and contemplation, I interpreted as growing up, growing pains.

According to Styron, the gloom that most people go through

and associate with the general hassle of everyday existence is so mild that it cannot give you a hint of the illness in its catastrophic form.

Michael's condition worsened in the second year of university. In his first year, he came out top five at Imperial College, where he was pursuing a mechanical engineering degree. It was known to be one of the hardest courses in the world, and of course, Imperial College was one of the top universities. The boy was undoubtedly a genius in my world. He came home boasting, and I did too. It felt so right to show off my son's achievement.

Six weeks later, he was back at university, and the worst of the disease began to manifest. His mind went blank, the luxury of concentration was lost, and his hands started shaking until he got to the point where he couldn't get out of bed.

'Mummy, I can't instruct my legs to move, to get out of bed. I feel like I'm paralysed.' He was low in the mornings, unable to move but felt better as the day went on.

As the disease progressed, his rhythm changed. By afternoons the gloom crowded in. He'd feel a sense of dread and alienation. Michael suffered from stifling anxiety, excruciating emotional pain and near paralysis most of his days.

This became his daily pattern the last years before his act. It took nine years, from 19 to 28 years old. Each attack got worse, but he often sprung back to life. Everything would be normal again until another episode.

After his first attack at 19, I returned with him to Zambia where he could relax and heal in the warmth of my bed. He could feel my love, closeness and sheer devotion. I loved him so much.

Many people told me that depression was not treatable. It was a grave illness that would only progress with age. I had to learn to live with it and to understand it. I felt one with my son. I wished I was the one afflicted with the illness. Why him? He was so young and had his whole life ahead of him. He felt like his mind was beginning to dissolve, and his distress intensified.

'I could have been top of my class, oh mummy. My life is a failure. I've ruined my life. I've fucked my life; what's happening to me?' he questioned, 'It feels like I'm losing my mind and all my talents.'

Tucked in bed at night, laughing and chatting, he healed relatively quickly. I understood it as love healing. A few months later, he was back at university, but his mental focus was never the same again. From a top student, he became average and struggled to complete his degree with flying colours. Flying colours was all he ever knew, and mediocrity was never for my boy.

He had memory lapses but pulled himself together to get a decent degree and took an extra year to complete his masters. He passed well but not with the distinctions he was accustomed to and it hurt him. We blamed it on his nervous breakdown. The awards went to others, something he had never experienced before.

He graduated with a master's degree from Imperial College, London, and returned home immediately. He hoped to take over or assist in his father's ailing business. His father would not have it. They had unnecessary fights, and feuds went on between them. I stopped getting involved and asked him to let go of his father and get on with his own affairs.

As the disease progressed, he developed anarchic disconnections, which Styron termed as bifurcation of mood. Mornings were lucid, he went to work and was excited about the different projects he got involved in. Then by afternoon and evening, his anxiety began to set in.

It seemed to me that life for him became a struggle and difficult. Sometimes he had panic attacks and appeared to be utterly disoriented. His thought processes, as described by Styron, 'Were engulfed by a toxic and untamable tide that obliterated any enjoyable response to the living world.' Instead of pleasure, he felt pain. He went out every night. He preferred noise to distract him and avoided being alone. The problem was that some months were spent that way and then suddenly, he would leap back into life. The depression appeared to have left him, and he was well.

I'd lived with his dad for 21 years. His father was prone to depression, constantly having his ups and downs, but he always seemed to lift himself out of it. I assumed that he had inherited the same pattern as his father, down for a period then filled with new energy.

I got used to their ups and downs, but at the age of about 27, everything changed for Michael. I was away, living by the lake, and I did not notice the massive change. I was not there to witness the final descent. Michael went on a suicidal high, where he became dangerous to himself and others too. He was incapable of being disciplined. He had a disregard for authority, including the police. He called himself 'godlike,' placing himself on a pedestal above others.

I travelled at the end of 2016 to pick him up and found him in indescribable pain, but at the same time, he was physically torturing himself. He did 100 to 200 pushups on his knuckles until they bled. I wondered whether he compensated for the emotional pain by torturing himself

He had no appetite and just nibbled at food. He didn't laugh anymore, he spoke less and got irritated when I talked to him. He said I talked too much. His mind was always distracted. When you asked him a question, he wasn't with you, and if he did try to answer, he mumbled. It irritated us all because we couldn't hear what he tried to say.

It's only going through Styron's book, in 2021, far too late, that I think for the first time, I truly grasped the depth of his pain. The author describes it as, 'An insidious meltdown of the mind, an upheaval, like your whole system is convulsing, like a howling tempest in the brain.'

Michael had always been a speed demon. He loved his cars and motorbikes. He also enjoyed jumping out of the sky. He was reckless and had ended up with many injuries— a broken hand, dislocated shoulder bone, and a fractured leg. What I understood from this book as, '… baring overtones of near-suicide and a flirtation with death.'

He was hurting so much, sometimes going around like a zombie. His eyes were blank, and his gaze changed. He looked drugged or tranquillised. His eyes had lost their sparkle and shine. His skin had broken in pimples. He kept squeezing and picking at them, worsening the situation.

Depression is clinically described as 'a disruption of the circadian cycle, the metabolic and glandular rhythms essential to everyday life.' Therefore, his alternating periods of intensity and relief were understandable. I guess, in many ways, I was in some denial about how deep he had fallen. I'd seen him bad before and return to normality. That time wasn't any different; with love, comfort and security of home, he'd come to life again, and all would be normal.

'The problem is,' I heard Peter say, him with his medical background, 'with each attack, his condition will only get worse.' We were going to get it sorted out. I never expected my son would ever commit suicide. Suicide, to most of us, lessens a man's character. Michael, I believed, would be the man who would grapple with the problem and come out to be the one who would help others with the same illness. This would become his gift one day; that's what I saw of him.

He had always been the group leader, and therefore, I saw this illness as his gift. It would be the very thing that would lead him to his purpose, of helping others with the same disease.

The situation was worse than I could imagine. Because of our denial, he was unjustly made to appear the wrongdoer and trouble maker.

I continue to write about him, and it's only now that I fully appreciate the level of his pain. Even today, I feel the guilt of not having explored and read more while he was still with us. I did not do much to understand him and the depth of his pain. 'Violent eruptions, fluctuations of mood, fits of black despondency, so devastating, you can no longer bear the pain, the nature of this pain is anguish you can no longer bear.' I read on.

I hated myself for not having researched more and looked at different options. Why did I trust one man's opinion, one psychiatrist and the only one in Lusaka? We should have flown to South Africa to get a second opinion.

According to Styron, 'Healing, time, medical intervention, where necessary, hospitalisation. In many cases, but most of all, the shame and secrecy to the subject. The taboos around mental illnesses would have to be cast aside.

So many souls are suffering from the same problem, depression, mood disorders, mental instability. Whatever we call it, mental illnesses are afflicting so many, manifesting themselves in different ways for each individual. It is so complex, impossible to define. All the mental distress people are going through.'

I began to understand that all the seeds of the illness had their strong roots in childhood, some shot into euphoric heights like my son. Others went straight down, a unipolar. My son was bipolar, swinging from ecstatic heights to suicidal lows.

According to Styron, the issues that led to suicide were sometimes accidents, people suffering from injuries, paralysis, who'd choose suicide instead of living with a defect.

However, failures, failure, being faced with too much criticism which you perceive as failure. A declining career, nasty reviews, and once again an inability to take criticism, which you perceive as failure.

Sometimes people committed suicide because they were caring for a loved one. Sometimes losing a loved one, all these incidents, as random as they may appear, situations that become a sore in the person's side all led to one's suicide. A torment, bowed by the outrages of life. Many stagger along on the down road, but others plunge straight down and choose the strategy of suicide.

I imagined my son to be a fighter, a fighter like his mother. He would come out the victor and lead the way. That was my optimistic thinking.

Michael's father was a depressive, and his aunt too. There was the genetic side as well, and finally, the trauma. Was it the divorce that caused the irreparable emotional havoc? Was it the emotional abuse from the father? Was it the loss of his doting mother? I had moved away to the lake and wasn't there as his daily comfort. A form of devotion from me that he'd always had, I was far away expecting him and his sisters to become independent. It may have been a combination of all these separate incidents put together that caused the downward spiral.

The more I read and researched about the illness, my guilt intensified. Why had I not done this before?
Styron continued, 'the body becomes frail, numb, an enervation, an odd fragility takes over, you become frail, hypersensitive, somehow disjointed and clumsy, lacking your normal coordination.... There are twitches, pains; the mind is going haywire, a fidgety recklessness keeping you on the move. There

is a daily erosion of mood, anxiety, agitation, an unfocused dread, immense aching and living in your own personal solitary place, solitude, concentration is difficult and exhausting, you start stalling, and finally, you cease.'

I recognised all this in Michael, but what was the point now? Why hadn't I done all this reading earlier? I should have looked for more books, materials and information.

'The dreadful, pouncing of seizures of anxiety, depression in its extreme form is madness! An organ in convulsion is the only description I could conjure in my mind. Loss, loss, in all its manifestations, appear to be the tombstone of depression.' Loss in childhood, loss of self-esteem, loss of self-worth, loss of self-reliance, all these could degenerate into infantile dread, dreading the loss of things and people, close and dear.

I turned to the only authority in Lusaka, the psychiatrist. I was told it would take about three to five months before he would calm down, but no one had explained to me. Afterwards, he'd be put on another drug to keep him on an even keel. I kept him on the drug for six months, giving him the smallest doses possible. Six months passed, and he seemed to be doing well. He was calm, manageable and able to talk. I chose to tell Michael that we'd been secretly medicating him. He was furious and refused to continue the medication. Within six weeks, he asked to meet the psychiatrist himself to ask for help. He wanted to feel better because he was going down fast.

He was put on Lithium to stabilise him. What we weren't told is that if he ever stopped taking the drug, it would take time, about three weeks at least before the drug would kick in again.

This was one vital mistake we should have been told and warned of. There was no instant, miracle medicine, each medicine would take time to settle, and even the dosage had to be monitored.

Once alone in London, he again stopped taking the drug and as usual it took him down. I discovered his medication after he had departed. It appeared that he had only taken three tablets. The rest remained untouched.

My son suffered from an acute fear of abandonment. He was afraid to be alone in the house and always wanted people around him. Friends slept over or went out for lunch. He couldn't be alone, yet I had left him alone in the London apartment.

I noticed he had developed fierce attachments. For instance, if you took his jar of Vaseline, he'd get annoyed. He was unusually jealous and possessive of his new girlfriend. Each item I learned, 'A reminder of a world soon to be obliterated.'

Every picture I took of him on our last trip together, when he smiled, his smile looked fake. Peter mentioned it, 'Why does he smile like that? It looks so false.' He had learnt to live with pain. I had learned to live in pain. We were taught from a young age that you held your pain to yourself. Some complain and whimper, according to your level of stoicism, but basically, I lived with my own pain, but his pain was unrelenting,

I cried, 'So late, so late, so late.'

'THE WALKING WOUNDED! It's a trial attempting to speak even a few words. It's despair beyond despair.'

Before the suicide, commonly experienced is a second half, the second half of yourself, 'an observer, watching with curiosity, as his or her companion struggles against the one coming disaster. In all of the suicide is a theatrical quality, as you prepare yourself for extinction, a sense of melodrama. The victim of self-murder, you are both the actor and the audience, and how you choose your mode of departure is all prepared, the message, the will, the letters, how you'll do it, all goes through the mind, it is all planned and prepared.'

The ones who escaped and came back to tell their story, what seems familiar to all, was a feeling of emergence from darkness to light, something or someone had saved them.

Could the medication have exaggerated the suicidal ideas, especially the medication we used to calm him down? Did I keep him on the downer for too long, which brought him so low, his only route out was suicide? I lived in guilt.

The stigma attached to mental illness frightened me. If I took him to Chainama Hills College Hospital in Lusaka, would he be labelled mad forever?

Should I have taken him to Johannesburg to seek medical advice or admitted him into a rehab centre where he could have had time to repose?

The safety by removing him out of the world, giving him time to rest. Getting him away from the competitive, the world of money and business, in a hospital or rehab centre, where he'd be allowed to rest, relax, be watched, be taken care of, detention, with only one purpose, one duty, to get better, to heal.

Did he need seclusion with me at the lake, where peace could return to his mind? Could I have done more?

For the ones who did get through mental illness and depression, whatever the case was, Styron narrates, 'It is a simulation of all the evil in our world, of our everyday discord and chaos, our irrationality, warfare and crime, torture and violence, our impulse toward death and our flight from it, held in the intolerable equipoise of history. You feel you want and deserve to perish.'

The saving grace I feel today is that it is curable. Some who have recovered feel like:

'An ascent, a trudging upwards, out of hell's black depth and emerging into the 'shining world' of life, a return to serenity and joy, having endured the despair beyond despair.'

My baby chose the light of the other world. I love you, Michael, is all I could say. I think of my love for my son, and with this love, I will be uplifted to live my last years in service of the creator. I was left with purpose; how that would manifest, I cannot tell, but I have to love and live again—a life with meaning.

I accessed my present life.

MARCH 2021

From January to March 2021, I had the lodge all to myself. I waited for the new management to take over.

How things had changed, I could now watch YouTube videos daily, and WhatsApp worked like magic. My friends Georgie, Gayathri, Renuka, Temsy and others had formed a group where we posted daily chats, pictures of each other, birthdays celebrated on the group, the days of letters and emails were long gone. My post box was abandoned, Box 43, Mpulungu, no longer existed, the post office closed down.

I could buy carrots, green beans, green peppers, apples, pineapple and sometimes watermelon at the market. Groceries were available, and a new Chinese shop had just opened, improving all our access to food. It was nothing luxurious, but everyday commodities were there.

In March 2021, I would have been at the lake for seven years. I was about to leave it to two capable, young managers. I had

had my life here, I had no plan to sell the place, but the daily running of a lodge took its toll on me. I had lost interest in the daily chores.

I still loved the people. I spent time at the clinic and school. Happy, the headman, came over for breakfast and told me the latest gossip of the place. The boatmen were preparing a new wooden dhow for me that I was in the process of negotiating a price.

Peter was diagnosed with throat cancer and had returned to Denmark. Joyce, Martin's partner, had also been diagnosed with throat cancer. She passed away later in August 2021, leaving Martin alone to manage the Waterfront. Strange how he had been so sure that she would be the first to go instead, it was Joyce, much younger and fitter than he was.

Morkell and Yolande continued to manage Isanga Bay. Hope settled in Serenje with her partner and one year later gave birth to a baby girl. Julie was happy at The Royal Zambezi taking care of two children, helping them in their early years of learning. When I needed a little gossip, I stopped in at Charity, sometimes spending the night at Nkupi and being picked up the next day by Thomas, my coxswain.

The students continued to visit. In spite of corona still visible and active, we had to wait to see how far this disease would go.

As for the Davy case, soon after my son passed over to the other side, I asked for an out of court settlement. I couldn't cope anymore. The settlement was a joke, but I wasn't ruffled at all. What I'd understood from life is that we pay. The Davy's and Andrew Howard might have won the battle with me, but you know, there's the eye of God, the eye of the creator watching. He, you can never crook. Their time would come, and oh my God, I may decide to pop a bottle of champagne, and I'm afraid it might taste too good. I wouldn't want to be in their place when karma calls.

The magic of the lake would never leave me. I was part of it, my thoughts deepening, my reflections, more profound. I felt, I hoped, I enjoyed thinking, contemplating, I loved my aloneness, my solitude, my oneness with nature. I felt one with the living cosmos. The connection with the Divine. I could feel the sensitivity to appreciate, to compliment, to admire and most of all, to love at such a deep level. This my son had taught me. I had no need to love one man anymore, one partner. I loved the world, I loved people.

In all our differences, we were so much the same. We cried, we suffered, we all wanted happier times.

We all needed each other. We all had the ability to care. At some deeper level, we are one and united, our exterior different, charmingly interesting, unique but in spirit, all one.

The lake had hit record-breaking levels, higher than had been seen for years, 1998, being the highest. This year was far beyond these levels. Every month was a bitter storm. My jetty was underwater. The little thatched deck we had our sundowners under was smashed down by a storm. The platform it sat on, all under. Boats filled with soil and showing off fresh blossoms, of cannas and bulbs, all taken by one Mpulungu storm.

The last storm took the paths leading to the chalets. I had foreseen this, opening up paths behind the chalets and creating an enchanting forest behind the main buildings and chalets. I spent my time in the forest, picking chanterelles. The more we opened and cleaned the thicket, the more mushrooms we found. Matata was delighted with the morning walks into the forest. It provided an alternative to the beach. You could still swim, but we had no beach.

I created picturesque and enchanting picnic spots in the forest, extending the paths into the new camping site. It could be used for camping and perhaps a grand festival, an annual art, cultural and spiritual festival.

A festival of life is something I was planning. My thoughts went wild planning the last chapter of my life, which I hoped was not going to be about running a lodge. I wanted others to do this for me so that I could focus on the creative and exciting things that life offered.

Kennedy and Becky arrived on 2 March. I had planned to spend the weekend with them. The weekend was filled with guests, which was the best time to train them. Once I was done with the training, I would be back on the road, saying goodbye to my seven years living on the lake.

The lodge was mine. The place was deep in my soul, the people dear to me. It was my second home. I knew I had to let go and allow new energy, young, and a dynamic team to take over while I moved to whatever it was God wanted of me. A new life, a renewed adventure, the next chapter, perhaps the last chapter of my life. It was going to be an exciting time ahead. I looked forward to getting home to Chinsali, knowing that-Mpulungu, Tukulungu and I were one in my heart and soul!

On my way back, Happy, the headman, travelled with me to

Kasama. He needed some medication for his diabetes from the chemist there, so I willingly took him along to buy whatever he needed.

On the journey, we laughed and chatted. I realised how close we had become and how deep our friendship had grown. I confessed that I was thinking of selling the place if things didn't improve. I'll never forget how his eyes jumped and turned to me, 'Vicky,' no longer 'madam.'

'Wipe those thoughts out of your head. We will fight, give whoever you want to sell to hell! We will never allow you to sell, never, Madam, (*suddenly, I was madam again*) stay here with us. We shall die together. No one will accept you to leave. You are ours, you belong to us, never, never again. Don't put those thoughts in your mind, please, never! We love you so much. We shall die together.'

I needed to hear that. We all need reassurance. To be acknowledged appreciated, in one way or other. The words came like magic, like pearls to my ears.

I was silent, inaudibly saying, 'I love you too, dearly, more than words can express.'